Barbara Mandel
17250 Parkland Dr
Cleveland Ohio

295-1133

Integrating Jerusalem Schools

This is a volume of

Quantitative Studies in Social Relations

Consulting Editor: Peter H. Rossi, University of Massachusetts, Amherst, Massachusetts

A complete list of titles in this series appears at the end of this volume.

Integrating Jerusalem Schools

Zev Klein

Department of Psychology and
School for Overseas Students
The Hebrew University of Jerusalem
Jerusalem, Israel

Yohanan Eshel

Department of Psychology
University of Haifa
Haifa, Israel

ACADEMIC PRESS
A Subsidiary of Harcourt Brace Jovanovich, Publishers
New York   London   Toronto   Sydney   San Francisco

ACADEMIC PRESS, INC.
111 Fifth Avenue, New York, New York 10003

United Kingdom Edition published by
ACADEMIC PRESS, INC. (LONDON) LTD.
24/28 Oval Road, London NW1 7DX

Library of Congress Cataloging in Publication Data

Klein, Zev.
    Integrating Jerusalem schools.

    Bibliography: p.
    Includes index.
    1. School integration— —Jerusalem— —Case
studies. 2. Jews, Oriental, in Jerusalem— —
Education— —Case studies. 3. Jerusalem— —Ethnic
relations— —Case studies. I. Eshel, Yohanan,
joint author. II. Title.
LC214.3.I73J474   370.19'34'0956944   80–1098
ISBN 0–12–413250–2

PRINTED IN THE UNITED STATES OF AMERICA

80 81 82 83   9 8 7 6 5 4 3 2 1

**For Nitza and Avram
who cared**

Contents

3
The Design of the Study   31

4
Integration and Achievement   51

5
Integration, Open Education, and Academic Performance   73

6
Academic Self-Concept   91

7
Social Interaction in the Integrated Classroom   109

8
Classroom Composition and the Activity-Oriented Method 123

9
Discussion 143

Preface

In this book, we report the results of a research project in school integration that encompassed more than 7000 elementary school children in Jerusalem. Israeli children from two distinct socioeconomic and ethnic backgrounds were integrated on a classroom-by-classroom basis, beginning with first grade. Their progress, as well as that of successive cohorts of entering pupils, was followed over a period of 5 years (1971-1975). The project, designed and implemented jointly by the Israel Ministry of Education and Culture, the Education Department of the Municipality of Jerusalem, and members of the Hebrew University faculty, was unique in several ways. It marked the first time that elementary school integration became a public and political issue in Israel. The project also included the introduction of a special form of classroom organization and practice intended to cope with the problems raised by integration. Additionally, the manner in which the project was implemented allowed for structuring a quasi-experimental design to evaluate its outcomes—a rarity in the research literature on integration.

Findings are presented and discussed separately for achievement, academic self-image, sociometric standing, and classroom observations. In each case, we have tried to relate the statistical analyses to a wide variety of classroom and system events that we came to know through personal observation and extended discussions with program participants. Moreover, the contrast between school integration in Israel and that in other countries, particularly the United States, offered a useful opportunity for uncovering a number of theoretical and practical issues often submerged in the highly charged atmosphere surrounding the subject. We hope, therefore, that this book will be of interest not only to researchers but also to those public officials, educational personnel, and parents for whom the figures we present and the events we describe reflect a deep and immediate concern.

Acknowledgments

In acknowledging all those who participated in making this study possible, thanks must go first to the principals, teachers, and supervisors of the Jerusalem schools in our study sample. Year after year, they patiently allowed us into their classrooms, spent long hours helping us with instrument development, answered our questions, and often were our guides in seeing what only an experienced eye might uncover in the special world of the classroom. We hope that what we have written does justice to their dedication, their perseverance, and the complexity of what they managed to create in the course of the project.

The Israel Ministry of Education and Culture provided both permission and support for us to carry out our study. The late Eliezer Jaffe was especially instrumental, as was the Office of the Chief Scientist and two of its incumbents, Ozer Schild and Shlomo Kugelmass. The Ford Foundation, through its grant No. B-2/7, was of major help in both carrying out and writing up the research.

Special thanks are due the National Council of Jewish Women Research Institute for Innovation in Education of the Hebrew University School of Education, particularly to its director, Chaim Adler, and Jane Cohen and Lorraine Gastwirt. They saw us through many hard times, and often gave us that small extra breathing space that enabled us to bring the study to completion.

Many assistants and students of the Hebrew University were involved in carrying out the research. Particular mention must be made of Ariela Brickner and Racheli Persitz, who shouldered a major part of the organizational task involved and contributed to conceptualizing various parts of the study. Mickey Frankovitz, Alicia Mackles, Avram Portnoy, Norman Wagenberg, Anita Schneier, and Moshe Cohen were especially helpful in the data analyses.

Our work benefited greatly from conversations and critical sessions held with many colleagues and friends. Of special note are James S. Coleman, Michael Inbar, and the members of the Inter-University Seminar on School Integration in Israel that met monthly during 1977-1978 with the support of the Ford Foundation.

The final sentences of acknowledgments are traditionally the place to thank our wives and families. Any words or phrases we might use would ring trite and empty. Our words could not make up for the upset schedules, the many hours away from home, the sequestered talking that often shut them out, the long silences, and other aspects of that underside of research that are rarely mentioned. For being part of this, and still smiling, we thank them.

1

Introduction

In examining the meaning of the term *integration*, Aahron Kleinberger (1973) noted that many uses of this concept in the social science literature rest on a biological analogy. An organism consists of a number of parts or subsystems, each distinct in both form and function. This differentiation, however, is in the service of an overall scheme of coordination. For the organism to grow and adapt, all parts must work together, the various differences orchestrated in such a way as to allow for both diversity and unity simultaneously. A threat to any part is a threat to the organism as a whole, whereas the integrity of a specific subsystem is dependent on its links and fit with all others.

These principles of unity in diversity, mutual interdependence, and coordination are at the heart of what, biologically speaking, is meant by integrated functioning. It is relatively easy to see in this model many of the meanings and allusions common to the analysis of interpersonal relationships and social structures. Cooperation and communication, resolution of differences, adherence to norms, cohesiveness, solidarity, conformity, and many aspects of socialization—all somehow call to mind the ideal image of a smoothly functioning, integrated organism. When applied to a real world of institutions, politics, and contending forces, it is a powerful image, able to touch upon some of the deepest feelings and longings that human beings have been able to set for themselves.

Like most images, however, it will not bear too close an examination. The same feelings and longings, as Kleinberger points out, can be put to a rigid and hierarchically organized caste system, unified under a single national banner, as well as to a pluralistic collection of individuals, each intent on his "own thing," loosely tied together by minimal adherence to some common goals. In a social context, integration is by no means an all-or-none concept, but represents a range of complex shadings and choices that can give rise to very different configurations.

The use of the term in the United States, for example, developed against a background of historical guilt and racial animosity, of rapidly increasing demands for equality, and an overriding principle of fairness within which many individual and group differences can be tolerated or even encouraged. In Israel, on the other hand, integration has taken much of its meaning from a central ideal of Zionist ideology—the in-gathering of the exiles. This refers to the creation of a national home for Jews from all over the world, often from radically different backgrounds and cultural traditions. All the various streams must somehow be blended into a new and united body, the undertaking given a special sense of poignancy and urgency by the continuous threat of war and destruction.

Again, powerful images and ideas, but suggestive of different problems and different solutions rather than a single unifying concept. It is a curious fact, however, that hardly any of these variations in meaning or their policy implications have been seriously examined in the literature on integration. Researchers and other writers tend to act as if definitions are understood and agreed upon. In fact, the only clear thing in common is a legal or administrative act called "integration," which is then identified as a goal in and of itself. Whatever more far-reaching aims may be associated with this act are only vaguely spoken of, the concern doubling back on itself to focus on the immediate events surrounding the act. There is an implied assumption that the "success" or "failure" of a particular instance of integration also says something about "success" or "failure" in some future version of society.

These differences in ways of talking about school integration cannot be simply or gracefully resolved. It might even be argued that it pays to keep things ambiguous, that social programs requiring wide-scale consensus and political support should not be defined too closely, particularly where ends are concerned. The danger always exists of getting bogged down in conflicting visions and aspirations to the point of blocking more immediate action. Furthermore, in order for ideological banners to unite and motivate, perhaps they had best remain nonspecific. The sources for the impetus behind many social action programs are not always the most rational (even when framed in the neutral languages of law or social science), and it is difficult to keep up the necessary head of steam when being coolly analytical and explicit.

It is not surprising, therefore, that the debate around school integration has been marked by extravagant desires and cruel disappointments, by minute attention to methodological detail as well as by curiously glaring omissions. The sense of something larger than life illuminates the discussion, but on a screen so wide as to make almost all interpretations possible. In the United States, school integration has been criticized for being an attempt to impose cultural homogeneity on recalcitrant minorities (Rist, 1970, 1978). In Israel, on the other hand, integrated classrooms have been attacked for being an improper setting in which to deal adequately with cognitive and emotional deficiencies of disadvantaged children (Frankenstein, 1976; Lamm, 1974). One observer, after reviewing the somewhat disappointing results of research in the field, concludes that immediate educational outcomes are of no special concern, while what matters is the "effort to make blacks and whites rethink their historic relationship to one another. If blacks and whites attend the same schools, then perhaps they will feel more of a stake in each other's well-being than they have in the past [Jencks, Smith, Acland, Bane, Cohen, Gintis, Heyns, & Michelson, 1972, p. 156]." The author is not very clear about how one goes about "making" racial groups reconsider their relationship, nor what going to school together has to do with this. What is conveyed is the sense of something desirable and important, yet strangely amorphous and suggestive, particularly as these statements are set in the context of a detailed statistical analysis that allows for very little ambiguity.

It is this marriage of political and ideological imperatives with methodological neutrality that creates the peculiar tension characteristic of the literature on school integration. To read, for example, the recent controversy of the actuality of a "white-flight" phenomenon (Frey, 1979; Pettigrew & Green, 1976; Rossell, 1978), with its masses of data, analyses, and re-analyses, is to realize that, along with the figures, a critical question the participants are demanding of one another is, "Which side are you on?" How this question is to be answered seems to be of equal if not more importance than the validity of any particular finding. One does not do research in the field of school integration without a certain consciousness that one is being personally as well as professionally tested. Nor is it clear, and perhaps it never will be, how much this consciousness and the pressure it creates are related to many of the unresolved problems and complexities of research in this field.

Another case in point is summed up by the authors of one of the most thorough and sophisticated studies of school desegregation. In dealing with their finding that 6 years of desegregation had no effect on the achievement of minority group pupils, they write: "The discovery that minority achievement is not automatically enhanced when minority and white children 'rub elbows' may be a disappointment, but on further reflection this expectation seems hopelessly naive, if not quixotic [Gerard & Miller, 1975, p. 298]." This one sentence quite accurately conveys the aura of "The Emperor's New Clothes" that has characterized much of the psychological reasoning behind integration programs and research.

Almost from the beginning, integration studies embodied certain assumptions both about how people change and the extent of change that might be expected from social intervention. Central among the assumptions has been the need for some form of major personality change leading to the acquisition of more achievement-oriented values, and the possibility of significantly raising achievement levels. Stripping aside the various ideas offered to explain how these changes might take place, the one mechanism counted on has been precisely the "elbow-rubbing" between minority and majority groups. And this despite the fact that most psychologists are well aware that even with the most powerful techniques available today, under highly controlled conditions, only modest results can be anticipated when trying to impact on personality or achievement. What Gerard and Miller call "hopelessly naive, if not quixotic" exactly sums up a situation where, for years, increasingly sophisticated methodological tools have been brought to bear on the search for phenomena that could, from another point of view, hardly be expected to exist. Perhaps no better example can be found of the interpenetration of two worlds—the political and the scientific—than school integration.

Throughout all of this debate the schools have continued to do more or less what they have always done, and what they are best equipped to do. Those changes brought about by integration programs (and this is true both of Israel and the United States) have mostly been felt at the organizational periphery of schooling, leaving much of the educational process itself unaffected. In all the accumulated literature on integration, very little can be found that deals directly with classroom procedures or curriculum changes. As Cohen and Garet (1975) point out, "while social action programs may seem like major accomplishments to their sponsors or advocates, such programs generally represent a modest change at the point of delivery [p. 28]."

The key word, of course, is *modest*, a term that can be applied equally well to the disparity between expectations and local implementation, and to what is known about the impact of schooling in general. These are the limiting conditions through which school integration programs must be examined and understood. By posing the question in the form, "Does integration work?" investigators have implicitly accepted all the complications and paradoxes, all the heavy significance of a social and political drama in which the day-to-day reality of the schools is but a single element, and perhaps not the most important. Moreover, asking the question in this way has not infrequently served to help divert attention from the difficulties and details of what might be done, if there were more careful attention to premises and greater concern for the actuality of classrooms, teachers, pupils, and schools. "Does integration work?" is a question that cannot be answered by social science alone, and probably should not be, since the answer must incorporate much of what a society would like to think of or imagine itself to be. Such answers are not reducible to methodologies or statistics, and can only arise from ongoing experience and debate within the society as it goes about defining and clarifying its own reality.

In the research report on a school integration program in Jerusalem that follows, we have tried to find a more appropriate way of joining this debate, still uncertain as it is being written of how it will be received and interpreted, but sure of the fact that the terms of discourse in which the project described was conceived must now be altered. We will have little to say about whether or not "true" integration was achieved, whether some new kind of collective identity was formed among the children, or if the effort expended was worthwhile by some measure of social or educational benefit. These are subjects for the debate in which we can be participants, not expert witnesses with definitive or final answers.

What we can talk about, and with more confidence than when we began, are the important elements in how schools try to carry out their mission with pupils of greatly different backgrounds and abilities. This is the everyday reality we followed for 6 years, and one we came to know with a degree of intimacy not often characteristic of research teams with their annual tests and reams of computer output. In many ways, the project was an embattled one. We often found ourselves the only ones available to listen to teachers, principals, parents, and school officials as they struggled to give shape and content to a vague mandate imposed on them with little notion of where to turn for help. We shared in the excitement of watching the development of a new kind of classroom operation, but also the deep frustration of seeing programs curtailed and frozen by bureaucratic impersonality. Not infrequently, we had to act as spokesmen and advocates for some of the schools as they fought to preserve a minimal degree of flexibility in ways of working with children. Most of all, we learned again, as Sarason (1971) put it, that "teaching is a lonely profession," a complex world often lost to view when dealing with it primarily as an independent variable to be coded and analyzed. We came to see only too clearly how terms like *commitment, creativity, dedication,* and *perseverance*, when applied to teachers, are fragile constructs with few sources of support.

The study, therefore, is less about the effectiveness of integration than it is about the way things happen in schools, and how the people within them, when given a chance, both succeed and fail at trying to make them better. In understanding their efforts, and in trying to define more specifically the conditions for success and failure, we may come a small step closer to relating the special world of the schools to versions of the future that are the best dreams of us all.

2

The Process of Integration

Jerusalem is a city of neighborhoods, each with a special identity of its own. In the late nineteenth century, Jewish settlers began moving outside the walls of the old city. They built homes close to one another in the natural pockets formed by rolling hills and deep valleys. Each new group found ways of putting a unique stamp on its part of the city. Often this was expressed architecturally, but even more so as a certain flavor, a style of life and behavior reinforced by the fact that these neighborhoods were, for the most part, either ethnically or ideologically homogeneous. Even as the city grew and the spaces in between gradually filled in, a sense of separateness and difference remained. This was to form a legacy of meaning and sensibility in which every new addition to the city would take part. Neither wars, nor a large influx of new immigrants, nor even the cultural levelling and uniformity characteristic of late twentieth-century living could totally undermine the nature of the city. When, in the 1950s, long, colorless blocks of apartments were put up rapidly to accommodate large numbers of families streaming into Israel from the Arabic-speaking countries of North

Africa and the Middle East, it seemed as if something might change. But these too quickly took on a name and atmosphere of their own—like all other neighborhoods in Jerusalem, a tangible expression of who one is and how one lives.

Historical Background of the Integration Program

This study begins with the story of two such neighborhoods. Both are old, as far as the recent history of Jerusalem goes, both physically near the center of the city, and divided from one another by a single street. With that, their resemblance ends; instead, their very proximity symbolizes many of the problems, conflicts, and paradoxes that mark the development of Israel as an independent state. One is a quiet area of tree-lined streets, carefully kept gardens, and large old houses, many built of massive stones that contribute to a sense of dignity and tradition. Few pedestrians can be found in this part of town, the life of most of the inhabitants focused on the special world indoors: high-ceilinged apartments, each with at least one wall completely filled with books; salons with the heavy, comfortable furniture of another era and another place; thick-carpeted rooms with large desks, set aside for studies; and always, the few tastefully placed original paintings or prints. It is not richness that characterizes this neighborhood. Rather, it is taste, dedication, and culture, in that original sense of the word which tried to convey a European ideal of how to conduct oneself and live one's life. The names on the doors are familiar to many Israelis, names of those who have contributed to the intellectual and political life of the country, some approaching the stature of national heroes. On almost any evening, many of these rooms will be filled with some of the most stimulating conversations to be had anywhere. In a country where extreme informality is the norm, on the Sabbath one can find formally dressed couples strolling here, occasionally lapsing from everyday Hebrew into the comfort of one of the European languages.

By contrast, the adjacent neighborhood is reminiscent of a typical Mediterranean town, stretching down the slope of a hill to where one almost expects a sea to be. The streets here are narrow and twisting, mostly open to the sun except for the intricate web of shaded alleys, walkways, and courtyards that connect everything into one complex unit. Houses are packed tightly together; balconies jut out over the street with lines stretched between, on which a daily display of laundry is hung. Above all, there are people: large families crammed into small rooms and spilling out into the street; small children running about; women calling to one another from their balconies, or pouring buckets of water over floors and steps, constantly scrubbing them clean. There are always boys and older men about—shouting, arguing, greeting one another, exchanging news of the day. In the background, radios are tuned to a mixture of pop music and complex oriental melodies. This same combination is reflected in the dress seen on the streets: the jeans of the young interspersed with long caftans, colorful scarves, the hooded robes of the Maghreb. Here Hebrew is interwoven with various North African dialects, the conversations mostly about family problems and gossip, making a living, and the endless details of dealing with bureaucracy.

The people in this neighborhood are what is known in the language of Israeli social science as "Jews of Asian–African origin," a catch-all term that includes an area stretching from Morocco and Tunisia to Iraq, Persia, and Kurdistan. In the Middle Ages, many of their ancestors were part of one of the greatest intellectual elites in Jewish history, synonymous with the rise and flowering of the Moslem Empire. The ensuing centuries, however, brought a general cultural, political, and social decay to the area. The Jews were reduced, for the most part,[1] to grinding poverty and almost feudal subservience. Events in the rest of the world generally passed them by; it was mainly the creation of the State of Israel in 1948 with the deep tremors this sent throughout the Arab world that stirred hope and movement that had long been dormant.

In one of the largest mass immigration programs of modern times, approximately 500,000 Jews were brought to Israel during the 1950s, almost doubling the population of the country in the space of a few years. The largest group in this rapid influx consisted of Jews from Arabic-speaking countries. What ensued is a complex piece of history that is still being written, and requires an analytical

[1]The history of the Asian–African Jewish communities is complex and variegated. Certainly not all of them were subjected to the same pressures, and many rose to positions of major governmental and economic prominence. (For a more extensive presentation, see Peres, 1971.)

scope that is beyond the limits of the present work.[2] We will instead try to present an indication of some of the feelings and attitudes that grew around the absorption of the new immigrants, a social atmosphere that is difficult to pin down but no less important than statistics and structural concerns in understanding the meaning of school integration in Israel. Feelings and attitudes tend to run to stereotypes, and thus distort and simplify. In what follows, this tendency will sometimes be exaggerated because the focus of interest—the two neighborhoods described above—is on almost opposite ends of a continuum. A large middle ground will hardly ever be referred to—in human terms, the many "oriental"[3] immigrants who rapidly and successfully merged into the general population, and whose numbers are constantly growing. By limiting our discussion to the more extreme cases, we run the risk of creating a false impression of the nature of Israeli society, which is nowhere as bitterly divided as the use of the terms *segregation, discrimination,* and *integration* in other parts of the world might indicate. Extremes highlight issues, however, and it is these issues and their resolution that form the context of this study.

Those who brought these new immigrants, who cared for their initial needs, provided them with jobs, housing, education, and services, and planned for their dispersal and assimilation into the country, were mostly of another history and another way of life. The settlers of predominantly European origin who brought the State of Israel into existence were the bearers of a rich and varied cultural tradition. In the 50 or so years prior to the establishment of the State, these settlers had experimented with transforming personal ideology into new social forms and institutions. The key theme in this development was *pioneering*, a complex term with both social and psychological referents. On the most personal level, it meant a commitment to self-transformation and change—a willingness to throw off restrictive traditions, and, above all, to act, in the certain

---

[2]Excellent analyses of this immigration and the absorption process can be found in Eisenstadt, 1967 and Shuval, 1963. The best account of how Israeli schools responded to a new and problematic pupil population is in Kleinberger, 1969. An up-to-date evaluation of the academic performance of children of Asian–African origin is in Minkovich, Davis, and Bashi, 1977.

[3]The term *oriental,* although geographically and culturally incorrect, is often applied to Israelis of Asian–African origin. It is a translation of the Hebrew word for *Eastern,* as opposed to *Western* and *European.*

belief that energy and intelligence could change the world in which one lives. This ideal became institutionalized in the emerging political and social structure of the country, and was an important element in the development of elites and centers of power.

Thus, when the immigrants from the Arabic-speaking countries arrived, they encountered a situation in which power, prestige, and status had already crystallized around certain groups with definite styles of life and ways of thinking, usually very different from their own. The older settlers were committed to the ideal of total absorption of the newcomers—indeed, felt it was crucial to the survival of the state. There was no particular awareness of "integration" as a problematic issue. However, the older settlers as a group began to close in on themselves, so that much of the openness and informality that had marked the process of immigrant absorption in earlier years was no longer in evidence. Instead, and in keeping with the functioning of a modern state, a large bureaucracy had sprung up. The new "oriental" immigrants became the passive recipients of government policies and actions—a complex and often impersonal machinery that presented an entirely new problem of adjustment. Services and allocation of living space were mostly segregated, so that the new immigrants often found themselves in discrete neighborhoods and isolated areas of the country, the low level of education and skills they brought with them placing them generally in the lowest of economic positions. They had all civil and political rights; most of their basic physical, social, and economic needs were taken care of; and a minor miracle had been accomplished in quickly absorbing them into the country. However, this absorption was at best partial, with the later and more difficult aspects of this process hardly thought of or dealt with. There was an assumption, not uncharacteristic of the pioneering ideology, that somehow things would take care of themselves, and that these new immigrants would find their way just as others had before them.

In the rapidly changing reality of Israel in the 1950s, however, this increasingly became a questionable assumption. The interplay of the traditions the "oriental" Jews brought with them and the particular conditions of absorption noted above tended to reinforce, rather than weaken, separate patterns of living and social identification. Lack of occupational mobility, poor educational performance, developing welfare needs, continued adherence to certain outward cultural forms (such as dress, style of interaction, even Hebrew pronunciation) all helped contribute to a mutual and uneasy distancing between the new immigrants and the older settlers. The expression "the two Israels" began to be heard, reflecting the disturbing consciousness that something had gone wrong, but also strengthening the tendency to confuse ethnic identification with social status. The collective goals to which all Israelis subscribed, and the universality of civil and political rights served to cover over the most obvious strains and tensions. At another level, however, peculiar stereotypes began to develop and became an important, if not very much talked about, element of the everyday life of the country.

For the older, established population with its European and Westernized outlook, the new immigrants began to take on features that have been imputed to lower classes everywhere. The "oriental" Jews came to be seen as lacking in drive and motivation; as passive, tradition-bound, and unable to function independently; and, inevitably, as a potentially dangerous source of social disorganization. The drive for modernization, accompanied by the fear of becoming "Levantinized," and thus indistinguishable from surrounding countries, lent particular impetus to these stereotypes. Theories were developed which pinpointed characteristics of the immigrants' family life and mentality that led to "primitive" functioning (one such theory closely associating the "oriental" style of life and thought with the Freudian id). These theories and ideas eventually gave rise to many concerted and important efforts to deal with the immigrants' many problems, but paradoxically, served to set them off even more as a distinct entity. One deep and often unexpressed fear was that of contagion, that the new immigrants in their large and constantly growing numbers might somehow seduce the establishment into a lowering of standards and levels of aspirations and achievement. This latter fear in particular plays an important role in understanding the meaning of the term *integration* when applied to Israeli schools.

The "oriental" Jews, for their part, developed stereotypes of their own. Most of them focused around a central theme of what they saw as a closed, increasingly affluent society, its members powerful and in control, dividing benefits and status mostly among themselves and making it very difficult for outsiders to gain access. The established settlers were all taken to speak Yiddish (a symbolic reference to the perceived in-group feeling among the older settlers) and to treat all outsiders with disdain and unconcern. They could be made fun of, ridiculed for their peculiar habits, strange accents, and bland European diet. They might be manipulated and, with enough cunning and ingenuity, even outmanoeuvred in gaining some particular advantage or benefit. But this was mainly a humorous covering for a deeply felt sense of alienation and resentment. The "oriental" Jews came to see much of their honor and self-respect as things left behind in their countries of origin, while in Israel they must be earned again, but in terms of reference that were strange, often unobtainable, and that almost always seemed to involve rejection of significant aspects of the self. They identified deeply with the country and its goals, but saw themselves continuously excluded from "making it" by powerful elites who were the arbiters of how to act and live.

Occasionally, these resentments spilled over into riots in low-income neighborhoods, demonstrations, bitter articles in literary journals, even organized political protest like the Israeli Black Panthers. For the most part, however, these outbursts were more cathartic than programmatic or constructive. Both sides had a major interest in keeping events balanced and more or less quiet. There was always the threat of war and external attack that demanded a maximum of internal harmony, and there was the hope, incorporated into all commonly held ideals, that with enough perseverance the situation would eventually change.

In part, all the foregoing helps explain the relationship between the two neighborhoods described at the beginning. The inhabitants of both might mingle on the street, stand together at bus stops, shop at many of the same local stores, and the men often serve in the same army units. Between them, however, there was a silence broken only in the privacy of one's home, with an unspoken agreement to act publicly as if the problem were recognized and being solved by those responsible. A rather benign lack of concern for those across the street pervaded the more settled neighborhood, sure of itself and its cultural hegemony.

It therefore came as something of a shock when, in 1966, an organized protest was launched by parents in the "oriental" quarter against segregation in the neighborhood elementary schools. For years, children of the two neighborhoods had attended separate schools, even though, in at least one instance, the buildings themselves were practically back-to-back. As far as the municipality, charged with apportioning school districts, was concerned this was not a consciously discriminatory policy. Instead, it accepted the "reality" of a situation where different children, of different talents, abilities, and backgrounds were held to be served best when educated more or less separately. The fact that the way children were allocated to schools almost perfectly reflected the social structure of the area was not discussed very often. What was clear was that, over time, at least two of the area schools had come to be known as among the very best in the city, whereas the others had a uniformly poor reputation.

Such situations usually develop a rhetorical dynamic of their own. The "good" schools were intent on maintaining their image in the community, and it seemed only proper and fitting to utilize a combination of parental pressure and administrative selection to include only those children suited for them. The "poor" schools, on the other hand, were the recipients of a great deal of sympathy and concern. The pupils in these schools were problematic, their parents seen as unsupportive, with school personnel feeling that they were doing the best they could under difficult circumstances. A combination of both resignation and devotion typified the staffs of the "poor" schools: Teachers were dedicated because the task of working with "oriental" children was important and closely linked to a major national aim. However, years of frustration and only minimal success led most teachers to feel that there were serious limits to what could be expected of these children. Beginning in the late 1950s, the Ministry of Education began to take cognizance of the fact that the children of the "oriental" immigrants presented a unique educational problem that would not resolve itself simply. Special compensatory programs designed to meet the needs of the disadvantaged pupils were introduced into the schools, particularly those like the "poor" ones in this area. A lack of sufficient preparation, supervision, and follow-up, however, almost always led to disappointment about the effectiveness of such programs. This, in turn, only strengthened convictions about what the children were actually capable of. Moreover, the teachers in the "poor" schools, as well as the "good" ones, were predominantly of European background, and thus closely identified with the attitudes incorporated into the way the school population was divided and perceived.

As mentioned earlier, behind the public stability in relationships between the two communities a deep reservoir of resentment and dissatisfaction had developed among the "oriental" immigrants.

For the most part unarticulated and unorganized, it was finally given a voice by a group of upwardly mobile parents in the low-income neighborhood whose personal experiences with attempting to better their positions became the occasion for organized protest. Better educated than other adults in the area, and often, like their spokesman, holding minor official jobs in the civil service bureaucracy, these particular parents began interpreting the status quo in a new light. Concerned both for themselves and their children's futures, they "saw" for the first time what had long been there to see: The school serving the poorer neighborhood was physically run-down, the services it offered were few in number, and hardly any of its graduates went on to academic high schools. Their first response to this changed perception was to try to provide something better for their children by applying for transfers into the more prestigious school. These requests were summarily rejected by the school authorities, thus setting the scene for translating personal problems and motives into public and ideological issues.

These parents then framed the idea of integration in the local schools, a concept so at odds with prevailing sentiments that, at first, hardly anyone in administrative control had any idea of what they were talking about. No consideration was given to the idea until public meetings began to be organized, and pamphlets and posters were circulated widely. An election year in Israel was also coming up. School integration was injected as a political issue with overtones of control over voting blocs and threats to party power. It was at this point that the seriousness of the issue was finally recognized and a joint Ministry of Education–Municipality of Jerusalem committee was set up to investigate the situation and make recommendations.

The committee began hearing testimony and investigated the situation in an atmosphere of rapidly growing public awareness, of pressures and counter-pressures. The parents of the low-income neighborhoods made every effort to give their case the widest possible publicity, any sign of rejection, delay, or procrastination met with escalating demands and threats of political and legal action. The parents of the prestige neighborhood, as well as the principal and teachers of the high-status schools in the area, were slower to react, but also began organizing. The pressures they applied tended to be subtler, aimed at high levels of both the municipality and the government through channels of political affiliation and personal influence. Publicly, this group issued statements emphasizing its commitment to an abstract ideal of social integration, but insisting that implementation at the level of elementary schools would be detrimental to all concerned and that "the time was not yet ripe." In effect, they suggested that school integration would lead to an educational and social disaster for both groups of children. Of special significance was the fact that they pointed out that no one really knew how to carry out integrated education, and that the Ministry could provide no educational tools to guarantee even a minimum of success.

When, in the early part of 1969, the committee issued its program for integrating the schools in the area, the result was a compromise that featured both an attempt to restore quiet and equilibrium and at the same time the introduction of new and risky possibilities. (See Chapter 3 for details of the program.) The parents in the "oriental" neighborhood had broken an uneasy silence and in so doing threatened to expose many of the contradictions between ideology and practice that marked the approach of the government and high-status groups in society to these immigrants. This was bound to cause a great deal of embarrassment. Government and municipality officials acted as had been done in similar instances: Under pressure, they gave in to the demand, but circumscribed it as much as possible, in this case by labeling and organizing the integration plan as an "experiment." This placed it as an isolated issue with no major reflection on wider policy. A special administrative structure was set up for the project that included representatives of the Ministry, the municipality, and the Hebrew University. This structure effectively isolated the program from all others in the Ministry, while simultaneously spreading the responsibility among many different sectors, so that no single person or agency could be held to blame.

Despite the public decision, no great hopes were held out for the program. Ministry of Education staff assigned to help out in the organization of the project were quite skeptical about the outcome, and privately predicted that within 2 or 3 years it would all be forgotten and the situation returned to "normal." They were also quite anxious to allay the fears of the high-status parents that their children would suffer in the experiment, or that this was the policy wave of the future. Several times during the first year of operation, high-ranking Ministry officials found occasion to announce that the experiment was not working, even when there was not the slightest bit of evidence on which to base this judgment. A major reason for not beginning the evaluation of the project until near the end of its second year was the fear that results would show that the achievement of middle-class children had been negatively affected.

Integration in this project was an ambivalent political act, built less on a strong commitment to the idea than on the needs of the moment. What helped sustain it was, on the one hand, the pride of the "oriental" community in having won their victory and thus the chance for their children to enter some of the most prestigious schools in the city. On the other hand, the middle-class parents, although afraid and angry, could not raise their voices too openly in opposition. To do so would mean publicly to go against a set of values central to the state and with which they were personally and collectively identified. Unable or unwilling to face this contradiction, they adopted, for the most part, a wait-and-see attitude. Educational and city officials were anxious to head off further difficulties from either side. They went on with the program while, at the outset, distancing themselves from clear responsibility or direction.

At least two important outcomes resulted from the way the project was initially structured. The "oriental" parents saw the decision as a way of furthering their thrust into the mainstream of Israel society. They were singularly unimpressed with arguments offered them about how their children would feel frustrated and incompetent in the newly mixed classes. It was obvious to them that their children would learn better and achieve more in the high-status schools, even though almost all the other actors—teachers, principals, officials, and middle-class parents—were highly skeptical about this possibility. The concern about achievement on both sides, however, shifted the focus very early on from integration as a political–social issue to an educational one. The test of whether or not the integration program was to be successful narrowed down to the issue of school achievement, even though a variety of other variables might have been chosen. The results of the 1966 Equality of Educational Opportunities Study (EEOS) in America were widely known in Israel, and its major finding of a correlation between classroom composition and minority achievement became an important feature of discussions around the project in Jerusalem. Thus, even though there was skepticism, there was also a growing hope that integration itself might serve as a new and powerful educational weapon. In effect, an association between administrative reshuffling of school populations and educational outcome was slowly being forged in the minds of officials and parents. This was to have a major impact on further developments in Jerusalem, as well as, more specifically, on the structure, interpretation, and use of the evaluation study.

Second, an interesting situation had come about in the target schools themselves. The Israeli school system is a highly centralized affair. Curriculum is closely specified and adhered to, scheduling and content is quite similar all over the country, and an extensive network of inspectors makes sure that not many deviations are allowed. Teachers are used to following directives and guidelines, and major individual initiatives, while not officially discouraged, are not particularly rewarded. As mentioned earlier, however, it seemed to the authors that school authorities were handling this project very gingerly, approving it officially but carefully maintaining a certain amount of distance and hedging on responsibility. The net effect on the target schools was that a vacuum in educational leadership was created. Teachers and principals found themselves suddenly with almost no one to turn to. Faced with the problem of having to deal with classrooms filled with pupils of widely varying abilities, they were confronted with a major threat to their feelings of competence as educators. Their immediate supervisors often acted as if there were no special problem, although it was obvious that handling the new situation would also require new tools and new approaches.

Impacts of the Integration Programs on the Schools

Almost paradoxically, the vacuum in authority provided a small but important opening for innovation and change. The executive group charged with administrative control of the project turned to several educators and university people for advice on how to carry out the integration program. Prominent among those contacted was the late Professor Avram Minkovich of the School of Education of the Hebrew University, a highly respected figure in teacher training, curriculum development, and educational theory in Israel. Among other accomplishments, he was the person most credited with introducing Piagetian concepts into Israeli education, and had played a major role in the design and implementation of the "New Math" curriculum in the country. Minkowich had written extensively about the active involvement of the pupil in the learning process, and was known as a major critic of many of the traditional teaching methods in Israeli schools.

When asked for advice, Minkovich laid down what he felt were some crucial dimensions of an ideal intervention for the integrated settings:

1. It must provide for maximizing individualized teacher–pupil contact in the classroom.
2. It must maintain the integrity and identity of the classroom group and provide for different needs and abilities without internal resegregation.
3. The teacher must have available a rich supply of materials and techniques with which to deal with the large differences among pupils.
4. It must be extensive, that is, continuous over all the years of elementary school with appropriate changes for age and curriculum demands.
5. It must allow the higher-ability and higher-status pupils to develop their own talents at their own pace.

This last point was particularly important, as Minkovich insisted that the "success" of the integration program would be measured not only by the achievement of the disadvantaged pupils, but by whether the parents of the prestige neighborhood were satisfied that their children were gaining something from the experience that was unavailable elsewhere. This, in turn, would have important bearing on whether or not the middle-class parents would come to support integration, or else begin to search out alternatives that would remove their children from the field and thus undermine the program.

In the 3 or 4 months remaining until the opening of the new school year, it was impossible to design and create an intervention meeting the above criteria. Minkovich instead suggested adopting the format of an already existing classroom innovation. Known as the *Kita Paaltanit,* or activity classroom, it had been developed and modestly employed for several years in scattered preschools and early primary grades. Its creators were senior preschool supervisors who had absorbed many ideas about the importance of the self-directed activity of the child to the learning process, and the consequent shift of the role of the teacher from authority to that of guide and facilitator. New curricula were already being experimented with that emphasized broad cognitive and personal development rather than the rote acquisition of specific skills. The curricula and teaching practices incorporated various concepts such as stages in cognitive growth, individual rates of development, the importance of intrinsic motivation through provision of choice and autonomy, and so forth. Major changes had been introduced into the classroom setting itself, mainly those involving the breakdown of formal classroom structure and the abundant provision of varied materials and projects, many supplied by the children themselves.

Those activity-based classrooms had been deployed almost exclusively in middle-class neighborhoods and schools, and there was no clear idea as to their suitability for the learning problems of disadvantaged children. Conceptually, however, they overlapped a great deal with the prescription proposed by Minkovich. By breaking down formal classroom relationships and structures, they provided more opportunities for teachers to work with individual children. Pupils would work on projects and tasks of their own, doing away with the need for uniform rates and standards. Informal task groups could come together and disband around many different activities, diminishing the need for strict division by ability level. Teachers would be freed to work with children most in need of assistance, while others could independently develop their own particular talents.

Equally important, the preschool supervisors who had helped create the activity-based classroom were a group of women with a mission. They saw themselves at the forefront not only of an educational innovation, but of a significantly different way of looking at and dealing with children. Their enthusiasm was infectious, and they grasped at every opportunity to implement their ideas. When invited by Minkovich and others to adapt their program for the newly formed integrated classes, they responded eagerly to the challenge. They rapidly planned a crash training program for the teachers who were to staff the new classes, and began cataloging the large amount of nonstandard material that would be required for such classrooms. The project executive committee quickly approved the idea of adopting the new classroom procedure, and allocated a considerable sum for the extra expense involved. An additional, and for the Israeli school system, revolutionary feature of this allocation was provision for a second half-time teacher in each newly constituted classroom (averaging 35 pupils). This was meant as an additional measure for increasing teacher–pupil contact and maximizing the impact on children in need of special attention.

Several aspects of this innovative development must be examined more closely. The loosening of centralized control over the project schools left room for trying out new ideas without the need to run the usual bureaucratic maze. Enough freedom of movement was created to allow teachers and principals to partially disengage from standard procedures, attitudes, and perceptions. Though this was initially anxiety-provoking, they were then offered a new approach which was optimistic in outlook and seemed to promise a way out of a difficult situation. This approach was taught to them by a charismatic, self-confident group of instructors who were not just giving them techniques, but inducting them into a special vanguard of educators identified with the new, the different, and the forward-looking. Concrete expression of this specialness was given by the extra materials and extra teaching staff allocated to the project, both major deviations from standard school procedures. In effect, the introduction of the activity-based classroom helped change the image of the project and its participants from that of an arbitrary, imposed solution to a social problem to one of an exciting and important educational experiment. During the ensuing years of the program, this image was constantly strengthened as the target schools became "showplaces" for visitors from all over the country, and were widely publicized in the press and on television.[4]

This "specialness" was not without its problems. The fact that the innovations introduced into the schools and the allocations supporting them were in the hands of an independent committee meant that the entire operation was somewhat outside regular channels. However, monetary support was tied to the annual budget of the Ministry of Education, and administrative definitions and routines of the Ministry still determined day-to-day operation. As long as the executive committee contained several high-level Ministry officials

---

[4]A detailed description of the initial phases of the project and an investigation of how the teachers assigned to it learned to cope with the new demands was done as part of a Master's thesis for the Department of Psychology, Hebrew University (Sherf, 1973). Another version of this work can be found in Binyamini and Sherf, 1977.

who were sympathetic to the program, problems of negotiation and control were not particularly evident. There was an illusion of compatibility between the needs of the program and the willingness of the Ministry to bend regulations in order to expedite matters. Personnel on the executive committee changed, however, and its composition shifted in the direction of lower-level administrators for whom the independence and uniqueness of the project were rather distasteful. The later years of the project saw a long series of discussions, debates, and negotiations as the Ministry attempted to reimpose routine definitions and rules, and the project schools fought a slowly losing battle to maintain what they had been promised at the beginning. Each year, with its new classes and expanded budgetary requirements, became an occasion for endless bargaining, one effect of which was to reduce the discussion to one of routine details of school operation rather than of educational inputs and goals. These negotiations also had the effect of adding another dimension to the questions being asked about the project, that of cost-effectiveness. The evaluation study that was carried out had no way of answering questions of this sort, but, as will be discussed later, the fact that such questions were raised helped provide a different focus for analyzing the data and interpreting the results.

Another problematic aspect of the intervention employed in this project stemmed from the ambiguous nature of its conceptualization. The preschool supervisors who identified themselves with the activity-based classroom saw it primarily in terms of a normative emphasis on the personal growth, development, and happiness of the young child. They had formed their ideas and techniques outside of the regular school framework,[5] and in many ways, saw themselves in an almost antithetical position to what generally took place in school. Though issues of cognitive development and learning were important to them, these issues were subordinate to a focus on the immediate activity and well-being of children, a special sense of caring with a long ideological history in preschool practice that verged on the therapeutic more than on the educational. It was a point of view that sometimes subtly, and sometimes openly, derogated what the supervisors felt was the school's lack of concern with

[5]Israeli kindergartens are housed in separate buildings, not directly connected to elementary schools. Supervisory and curriculum staff are a separate unit within the Ministry of Education.

the individual child and its overemphasis on standard achievement and results. Furthermore, the role demanded of teachers employing the intervention was itself complex and not clearly defined. Much depended on a sensitive appreciation of the changing needs of children, the talent and time to convert such "diagnoses" into appropriate materials and activities, and the opportunity to upgrade continually one's professional knowledge as a teacher.

The university consultants to the project, however, while sympathetic to the overall image of the activity-based classrooms, were primarily concerned with its usefulness as a vehicle for enhancing what schools normally teach, rather than as an end in itself. The problem for them was to translate expectations for achievement into methods that would allow all children to progress at rates compatible with usual school standards—even more so in the case of the disadvantaged child. It was a subtle difference in definition, but enough to be involved in causing the major university consultant to leave the program in its first year when not given total control over the operation of the intervention. The supervisors and participating teachers were, in an important sense, then left to fend for themselves, for there was very little help or advice to be had anywhere else in the country. Beyond their initial involvement in setting up the program and beginning the training of the teachers, moreover, the preschool supervisors had little more to offer. Their own time was seriously limited by other duties and functions, nor did they have much to say about how the intervention would be implemented in the higher elementary grades with their increasingly complex curricular demands.

A situation was created in which the participating teachers literally had to create much of the intervention out of their own imaginations. This included organizing materials, preparing curricula, discarding and revising techniques, and eventually, themselves doing the training and supervision of new teachers as successive waves of children entered the project each year. Motivationally, this concentration of responsibility in the hands of the teachers probably helps explain the enthusiasm and energy generated among the teachers and generally characteristic of their activity throughout the project.[6] However, it also meant that there was always the question of how much more effective the project might have been if

---

[6]See Binyamini and Sherf, 1977.

provided with professional and technical assistance. There was no way of knowing if errors in either concept or practice had become built in over time, or if the overall meaning of the intervention had become subverted as educational issues in the upper grades became more salient. Teachers might be mechanically applying a few simple techniques without grasping the multidimensional nature of the role required. Or, depending both on school context and differential emphasis, they may have been exaggerating one aspect of the program to the detriment of another—for example, giving prominence to the "therapeutic" coloring of the intervention mentioned earlier and thus downplaying achievement. Whereas this would probably have little effect on the middle-class children, it might have interesting consequences for the performance of disadvantaged pupils (see Chapter 5). In any event, many different questions can be raised about the actual process of putting the intervention into practice, only some of which can be answered by the classroom observations carried out as part of the evaluation study.

On another level, the activity-based classroom quickly gained political and administrative significance very different from the problems of day-to-day implementation. Anyone visiting these classrooms as the project got under way could not help but be impressed. The enthusiasm and interest of teachers and children along with the greatly changed classroom surroundings conveyed a sense of difference and impact that, by contrast to what usually took place in schools, seemed to offer an optimistic solution to many difficulties. It was not lost on educational officials that high-income parents of pupils in the project began breathing easier as they saw their children enjoying themselves and evidently gaining a great deal from their school experience. Nor did it take long to realize how proud the disadvantaged parents were of the fact that their children were participating in a high-prestige operation. (Stories circulated about these parents locking first-graders into their rooms after school to make sure they were doing their homework, and thus ensuring continued participation in the project.)

In parallel, principals of other schools in Jerusalem saw that the deployment of the new intervention meant additional funds, salaried positions, and a not inconsiderable amount of prestige by being associated with a new approach to education. At about the same time, the Ministry of Education, as part of a series of moves designed to decentralize control, began allocating discretionary funds to schools, with which principals were free to carry out their own pet ideas and innovations. The activity-based classroom was an obvious choice, made all the more salient by the attention increasingly being paid to the integration project schools. Moreover, other groups of low-income parents in Jerusalem were beginning to raise their voices about the quality of education their children were receiving. Taking their cue from the "oriental" parents whose protests had led to the integration project, these new groups were demanding improvements in neighborhood schools and raising politically embarrassing questions about the overall system of pupil allocation and district apportionment. Some way had to be found to placate this rising tide of resentment, as far as school officials were concerned, in a way that would both have high visibility and offer the promise of educational change.

One result of all these pressures was the transformation of the *idea* of the activity-based classroom from one of an experimental innovation, still unproven and still developing, to that of a ready technique for dealing with organizational and political issues. Solutions had to be found quickly and presented with a degree of certainty that was hardly compatible with any careful and slow examination of results. Within 3 years after the program had begun, Jerusalem schools were literally flooded with activity-based classrooms, most of them hurriedly thrown together, with only the barest minimum of teacher acceptance of preparation, and in a wide variety of schools, ranging from the best to the worst in the city. Supervision and follow-up were almost nonexistent for these new classrooms, their main currency deriving from the simple fact that they now *were*, and thus meant to imply that significant change had taken place.

The educational meaning of this rapid expansion is a subject for separate discussion. Administratively, however, the activity-based classroom had now become an issue unto itself. It had originally been brought into the project as a framework for maintaining integrated classroom groupings and providing a means for more effectively carrying out educational goals within such settings. The developments noted above, however, had the effect of at least partially splitting off the activity-based classroom from its link with integration, forgetting for the moment that much of the enthusiasm it generated had come precisely from such an association. The intervention began to be seen, particularly by school officials, as an indepen-

dently powerful technique that, if one listened carefully to the way
it was often described and promoted, held out almost the promise of
a miracle cure for the learning problems of the disadvantaged. Aside
from the immediate capital of making such promises, this had the
effect of clouding over many political issues associated with the
integration of other Jerusalem schools, as well as educational issues
involved in the proper implementation of the intervention. What
then crystallized as a further question for the evaluation study was
"To what extent could the activity-based classroom stand alone as a
method for improving the school achievement of disadvantaged
pupils?" The answer to this question would be important not only
educationally but politically as well, by seemingly offering an alternative to all the conflicting pressures involved in the physical act of
school integration.

Asking the question in this way, however, and offering such
alternatives paradoxically reinforced a tendency to see school integration by itself as a technique that could lead to better outcomes for
the disadvantaged. Lower-income parents pressuring for change
generally focused their attention on schools, not the programs
within them. Though the promise of better education for their children was interesting and important, its main association was with
type and population of the school, and only secondarily with what
was taking place in the classroom. As more and more lower-income
parent groups began pressing for school integration a shift in policy
became noticeable among municipality and ministry officials. In
1969, integration was almost grudgingly accepted, and with little
hope of success. By the early 1970s, however, integration was
rapidly becoming a major issue in the community at large, and the
"establishment" was taking note of it as it had rarely done before.[7]
For whatever complex political reasons, officials were now ready to
come down squarely on the side of elementary school integration. In
the debates and discussions that followed, the political necessity of

---

[7]Several factors contributed to this change, some local, some national. Perhaps
the most important event to bring school integration into public prominence was the
School Reform of 1969, which created a new system of comprehensive junior high
schools. An explicit justification for this reform was to promote social integration
among school children, and by implication, in the country as a whole. In Jerusalem,
this reform had been tested in the courts by middle-class parents who refused to send
their children to the new schools, insisting that the choice of school was theirs. The
parents lost their suit in highly publicized court decisions.

such a policy was often linked with the possibility of its educational benefits, even though there was very little evidence to support this conjecture. This was also a period of major cuts in government spending which limited the money available for special programming in the schools. Thus, an administrative solution which would not require much additional expenditure gained major attractiveness when compared to a relatively expensive intervention like the activity-based classroom. This dissociation between integration and the intervention was further aided by the fact that the municipality was responsible for one (school districting) and the Ministry of Education the other (classroom content and instruction), with coordination and agreement between these two authorities not always optimal.

One outcome of this growing reification of elements taken to be integral at the outset of the project has already been noted: With each successive year, the project schools had to fight more difficult administrative battles to try and preserve their educational program in the format originally planned. School authorities, on the other hand, were engaged in trying to deal with a rapidly changing community situation, using whatever tools were at hand to offer compromises and play down conflict. The need for quick results led the authorities to propose now one and now the other alternative, heightening the feeling that integration and the activity-based classroom were of equal value in affecting the disadvantaged pupil.

All these events helped sharpen and focus the questions being asked in the evaluation study. The research team had originally undertaken to help answer some simply framed questions about the outcomes of a relatively discrete project in a community where it represented a unique departure from usual social organization and educational practice. As the project developed, however, the community at large was also changing, events having impact both on how the project was carried out from year to year and on the significance of the project's various components when placed in different contexts. Simple questions that assumed stability of both inputs and outcomes rapidly became inadequate as a way of formulating what was taking place. Instead, the problem had become one of trying to define more closely the necessary and sufficient conditions of "success" for any particular strategy linked to the various options that grew out of the project itself and the changing school situation in Jerusalem. This does not mean that the design of the study was changed from year to year. It does mean that the research team's own perspective on the study was inevitably shaped by events transpiring both in and out of the project. Teachers came and went, were elated or depressed; principals fought for what they believed in, or passively accepted what they took to be the inevitable workings of bureaucracy; middle-income parents around the city were increasingly put on the defensive, while lower-income parents were becoming more open in their demands, both looking for facts and figures to support their positions; school officials manoeuvred to find ways to resolve conflicting interests; policies were created, dropped, subverted, or replaced in rapid succession; experiments became slogans, and slogans turned into operational rules. All these events forced the research team increasingly to turn their attention to what went on inside the "black box" of the project and its various spin-offs. They came to see school integration as a fragile human invention, born out of political and social need, uneasily wedded to a possibility of educational benefit, and subjected to all the currents of influence and ideology characteristic of a rapidly changing community. The report that follows is a modest and necessarily incomplete attempt to set the project in context, perhaps making the options a little clearer.

Afterword

In the summer of 1977, 8 years after the project had been begun, the mayor of Jerusalem publicly announced that *the* major issue for the city's schools in the near future was that of integration. Several months earlier, the vice-mayor in charge of the educational portfolio in the municipality had spoken openly about the end of the concept of neighborhood schools in Jerusalem. The director-general of the Ministry of Education stated in a newspaper interview that school integration must be effected at any price, even it if meant temporarily lowering the achievement of middle-class children. In the last national elections, almost every political party made the need for increased social integration a major element of its platform. The most comprehensive study ever done of Israeli schools (Minkovich, Davis, & Bashi, 1977) had just been published, with a relatively minor chapter on the effects of school integration singled out for wide dissemination in the press and debate in the Israeli parliament. As the new school year approached, a rash of projected parent strikes across the country was being reported on daily, all having to do with some form of a controversial integration plan. Here and there, parent groups were beginning to organize private schools to keep their children out of the system. It was a long way from 1969 and an isolated project in Jerusalem.

3

The Design of the Study

In summary, then, the improvement of research has had paradoxical results. On one hand, we have a less simple-minded and more plausible
account of social reality. Artifacts are reduced, distortions due to faulty
method are often eliminated, overblown interpretations are corrected, and
more careful analyses are presented. The technical sophistication of recent
research on desegregation is such as to inspire more confidence than 20
years ago that the results of any given study are valid. But these changes
have led to more studies that disagree, to more qualified conclusions, more
arguments, and more arcane reports and unintelligible results. If any
given study is more valid, the inferences to policy from the lot seem much
more uncertain [Cohen & Weiss, 1977, p. 407].

The argument presented by Cohen and Weiss and generally
substantiated by major reviews of the school integration literature
(St. John, 1975; Stephan, 1978) must haunt all researchers who set
out to design yet a further study. More data and better analyses may
lead to a more honest appreciation of real-world complexity. But are
relevant issues being pinpointed, or does the increase in sophistication lead to a situation where the object of all this study will "now
dance through all this like a will-o-the-wisp, appearing in some

studies and under some conditions and not appearing in others [Cohen & Weiss, 1977, p. 403]?"

In designing the present study, the authors were particularly mindful of one aspect of this problem: the growing concern with the pitfalls and artifacts threatening the validity of conclusions drawn from large-scale surveys. Such surveys, basically descriptive in nature, cannot answer many questions concerning the facts they contain, even though approximating such answers is critically important for reasons of both theory and application. In integration research, the advantages of large-scale representative samples in various surveys have been clouded over by serious deficiencies stemming from lack of control over relevant variables such as pupil self-selection, and various relationships of parental status, school location, quality of teachers, and student body with academic outcomes (St. John, 1975). A more rigorous experimental design seemed warranted, for which at least two major strategies have been suggested.

The first centers around the difficulty of matching experimental and control groups because of differences in baseline measures, growth rates, regression artifacts, and testing biases. A long series of theoretical and experimental studies by Campbell and his associates analyzed problems of internal and external validity in quasi-experimental designs (Campbell & Boruch,1975). Their conclusion was that several common sources of sampling biases are prevalent in almost every quasi-experimental design, often making their conclusions unverifiable. Therefore, "collectively, these biases and the inventions and assumptions required to correct them cumulate as powerful arguments for randomized assignment to treatments—for true experiments rather than quasi-experiments [p. 58]."

A second approach held that a breakthrough in studying multifaceted problems would require taking into account a great number of interacting variables rather than assuming that they are held constant through randomized sampling. According to this reasoning, unravelling these interactions may be the key to a better understanding of important factors affecting educational outcomes. It may also help explain incompatible results found in studies overlooking these interactions.

Two somewhat different conclusions were drawn from this belief in the prime importance of analyzing complex designs containing reciprocal relationships. One is held by Cronbach (1975), the other advocated by Bronfenbrenner (1977). Cronbach questioned the aspiration to reduce behavior to general rules. He claimed that higher-order interactions are required to account for most psychological phenomena. Since no proper methods of analyzing such data have been developed so far, he advocated a different strategy for educational research. Most of the theoretical models studying complex human phenomena have been based on linear relationships and on rather simple interactions. If it is true that higher-order interactions are required to account for the rich phenomena studied by psychologists, then every generalization is by definition temporary, representing an existing situation in a specific time in a changing universe, rather than a general rule. The "half-life" of empirical propositions will depend, according to this reasoning, on the ingenuity of the researcher in identifying local effects stemming from uncontrolled conditions. When local conditions are given proper weight, any generalization becomes a working hypothesis rather than a conclusion, and no simple application or translation of the rule to another setting is justified. Cronbach strongly suggests that rather than limiting oneself to answering formal questions stated in advance using either the experimental control or the systematic correlation method, the psychologist should use "intensive local observation [which] goes beyond discipline to an open-eyed, open-minded appreciation of the surprises nature deposits in the investigative net [Cronbach, 1975, p. 125]."

A similar feeling concerning the inadequacy and the futility of recent methodology in dealing with relevant social phenomena led Bronfenbrenner to suggest a new kind of "experimental ecology." He agreed that the ultimate aim of the required psychological experiment is discovery rather than verification, and that experiments should be employed not only for the usual objective of testing hypotheses but rather for heuristic purposes. Bronfenbrenner, however, went further in assuming that this effort will lead eventually to a systematic analysis of the nature of the existing accommodation between the person and the surrounding milieu, and to establishing new generalizations. In order to achieve this end, ecological research seeks to "control in" as many variables as possible, rather than investigate a single variable while "controlling out" all other interfering variables. A meaningful description of the reciprocal relationship between the person and his environment will require that "environmental structures and the processes taking place within and between them, must be viewed as interdependent and must be analysed in systems terms [Bronfenbrenner, 1977, p. 518]."

The study presented here was an approximation of an experimental (rather than a survey) design, based upon the actual possibilities provided by the project and the existing school system. We did not consider going so far as to despair of empirical examination of educational outcomes because of many unaccounted for interactions. Nor did we find an optimal way for "controlling in" all possibly relevant systemic factors. Instead, we took advantage of a unique community situation that enabled us to relate the effects of integration and open education to a variety of different outcomes. This was done by building a nearly complete $2 \times 2 \times 2$ factorial design with the following dimensions: integrated versus nonintegrated classrooms; "open" versus conventional methods of teaching; and low socioeconomic status (SES) versus high socioeconomic status pupil background.

The administrative plan that set the project into motion originally called for the inclusion of four schools. Two of these schools were populated almost completely by high-SES pupils and enjoyed a fine reputation for their high educational standards. Under the integration plan, first-grade low-SES pupils from the low-income neighborhood were integrated into these schools on a classroom-by-classroom basis. In each successive year of the project, new first-graders were incorporated so that eventually all children in all the elementary grades would be experiencing integration from the beginning of their school careers. The proportion of high-SES to low-SES children in each classroom was originally set at 60% to 40% and efforts were made by the administration to maintain these figures over the years of the project.

The other two schools originally in the project were composed almost exclusively of low-SES pupils, and were situated in the vicinity of the disadvantaged neighborhood. These schools were included primarily out of public and political considerations: All the children from the low-income neighborhood could not immediately be redistricted into two integrated schools. But the schools attended by the pupils had to be visibly recompensed in some way. The solution was to provide them with financial and programmatic support, similar to that available in the integrated schools.

An important component of this additional support was the

Kita Pe'altanit, loosely translated as the "activity-oriented classroom." Physically, these are similar to the infant school arrangement in England, or variations of the "open classroom" in the United States. Children sit and work in small groups, there is a fair amount of freedom of movement, and direct frontal teaching is minimized. Provision is made for the self-directed activity of the learner, the encouragement of spontaneous interest, curricular implementation of theoretical ideas about the course of the child's cognitive and emotional development, and greater opportunity for individual teacher–pupil contact and planning. Additionally, a second teacher was assigned to all project classrooms for a number of hours per week so as to extend individualized contact with pupils. From first grade on, all the project schools were accordingly provided with extra teachers, extra materials, and added in-service training. Potentially, at least, these additions promised a richer learning environment and more numerous pupil–teacher interactions. (See Chapters 5 and 8 for additional details.)

By the time the evaluation study was undertaken—in the second year of the project—the program of integration begun in the target neighborhoods was slowly spreading to other parts of Jerusalem as well. As a result, control schools could be selected to match as closely as possible the original four project schools. Integration of low and high SES children in control schools was not totally planned and was not supplemented with the activity-classroom intervention. However, integration was carried out on a neighborhood basis and without the necessity for any form of busing—exactly the same case as in the project schools.

Project and control schools were matched on the following dimensions: pupil characteristics (to be detailed more fully in the next section); status and reputation in the community, as judged by principals, supervisors, parents, and teachers; religious or secular affiliation; and academic level. The last presented a problem, since up until recently there were no standardized tests employed in Israeli schools. The only available measure was a nation-wide test, since discontinued, given at the end of elementary school in order to determine individual eligibility for state financial aid for high school education. The mean score on this test (called the *seker* in Hebrew) achieved by pupils in a given school was taken as an approximation of the academic level of that school, assuming a certain amount of stability in pupil and teacher population.

A comparison of the mean achievement of project and control schools in this fashion indicated a general similarity between them. Control schools found to be dissimilar were replaced by other schools after the first year of the study.

Pupil Characteristics and Subgroups

The characterization of a school as either integrated or homogeneous, on the one hand, or as activity-oriented or conventional on the other was straightforward. However, defining groups of children as either disadvantaged or advantaged presented some problems. As pointed out in Chapter 2, school failure in Israel is highly correlated with Asian-African origin. The Ministry of Education and Culture has incorporated country of origin among the major criteria for defining the disadvantaged. This was done in order to guarantee increased resources for uplifting a certain population as much as for objective scientific reasons.

In fact, however, school failure in Israel has been found repeatedly to be contingent on a number of background variables (Eshel, in press; Minkovich *et al.*, 1977), the most important of which is parents' education. Other variables add smaller contributions to the explained variance. Our interest in this study was to examine the impact of integration and a special educational intervention on those pupils who were presumably benefitting least from schooling. The strategy chosen was to focus on those pupils who, by the schools' own definition, are hardest to teach versus *all* others. Thus, all pupils were classified as either lower-class or middle-class. Pupils whose fathers had no more than 8 years of formal schooling and blue-collar occupational status, and whose families originated from the Asian-African countries were designated lower-class (LC). Pupils of *either* Asian-African or European-American origin, but whose fathers held white-collar positions and had more than eighth-grade educations were defined as middle-class (MC). In order to maintain the sharpness of this division, all children for whom the data were either unavailable or equivocal in terms of the criteria were dropped from the analyses (slightly less than 1% of the total study population).

By combining schools and subgroup affiliations, the following eight categories were constituted for the study:

MIP: Middle-class pupils studying in integrated classrooms using the "activity-oriented" method.

MI: Middle-class pupils studying in integrated classrooms using conventional teaching methods.

MP: Middle-class pupils studying in homogeneous MC classrooms using the "activity-oriented" method.

M: Middle-class pupils studying in homogeneous MC classrooms using conventional teaching methods.

LIP: Lower-class pupils studying in integrated classrooms using the "activity-oriented" method.

LI: Lower-class pupils studying in integrated classrooms using conventional teaching methods.

LP: Lower-class pupils studying in homogeneous LC classrooms using the "activity-oriented" method.

L: Lower-class pupils studying in homogeneous LC classrooms using conventional teaching methods.

The study began with 35 classes and 897 pupils in the 1971 cohort, and when terminated in 1975 included 167 classes and 4405 pupils. A detailed distribution of the various LC and MC subgroups in each of the study years is presented in Table 3.1.

Pupil and Classroom Comparison

The selection of similar control schools was based on judgments made by educational officials and others in the community. However, a major question in any form of experimental design is the extent to which experimental and control groups are truly equivalent. No perfect matching can be expected to be maintained in a dynamic school system over a period of 5 years, even when there are no drastic changes in the population or teaching staff. Changes in political and economic conditions or in educational policy may, among other factors, influence school enrollment in unpredictable ways.

The best comparison among the subgroups would have been some form of pretest before entering school. Such testing was not, however, carried out, and pupils were compared instead on the basis

The Design of the Study

TABLE 3.1
Distribution of Total Study Sample: Type of School, SES, Grade Level, and Academic Year

Year	Grade	Type of school								Totals
		LIP	LI	LP	L	MIP	MI	MP	M	
1971	1	73	47	121	64	119	52	—	—	476
	2	59	37	55	95	109	66	—	—	421
										897
1972	1	68	79	95	31	147	111	—	193	694
	2	70	37	100	25	122	68	—	207	629
	3	60	49	81	41	118	82	—	193	624
										1947
1973	1	73	99	53	72	152	201	—	254	904
	2	64	88	82	45	125	176	—	244	824
	3	68	46	94	54	139	114	—	249	764
	4	53	6	67	82	100	15	—	247	570
										3062
1974	1	64	67	62	49	158	152	32	119	703
	2	70	98	55	72	147	197	23	150	812
	3	65	94	77	73	150	183	26	145	813
	4	67	57	89	50	146	182	26	141	758
	5	57	26	97	76	161	183	—	132	732
										3818
1975	1	57	41	46	68	173	185	20	101	691
	2	52	61	62	63	164	160	30	99	691
	3	60	86	67	69	145	192	26	144	789
	4	61	67	78	80	142	191	25	132	776
	5	63	52	84	57	144	177	27	137	741
	6	54	24	93	87	160	173	—	126	717
										4405
									TOTAL	14,129

of their background characteristics obtained when they entered first grade. Although far from completely satisfying as a measure, it seemed reasonable to aim for a general similarity in background characteristics of the various subgroups replicated over the years of the study. A qualified equivalence among comparable subgroups might be assumed if whatever differences exist do not represent a consistent bias in favor of one or another subgroup. Table 3.2 presents a comparison of background characteristics for all MC and LC subgroups.[1]

Several significant differences can be found in Table 3.2. However, they are neither large nor consistent—no one particular subgroup seems to be affected more than any other. For the most part, subgroups appear comparable and maintain their comparability over the years of the study.

Even with comparability of pupil subgroups, a problem remains in composing classrooms—in particular, those designated as integrated. Research has shown (McPartland, 1969) that if integration does have any impact on outcomes, it is associated with classroom, not school, population patterns. The fact that a school is declared integrated and has an overall balanced enrollment is not always reflected in specific classroom organization. For various reasons, sometimes intentional and sometimes not, some classrooms become heavily biased toward one subgroup or the other. In elementary schools this tendency is particularly pronounced in the upper grades as curriculum demands become more difficult.

It was decided, therefore, to adhere stringently to a *classroom* definition of integration, and retain in the study only those pupils who enrolled and continued to learn in classrooms that met specific criteria. Integrated classrooms were defined as those containing no more than 60–80% MC pupils and no less than 20–40% LC pupils in schools designated as integrated. Homogeneous classrooms were defined as those containing no more than 10% of either LC or MC pupils in schools designated as homogeneous. Classes which did not fit this definition were discarded from the sample.

Test Measures

Three areas of outcome were investigated: school achievement, self-image, and sociometric status.

[1]No data were available for LI and MI pupils separately. The MP group was derived from an experimental school that did not include a seventh grade. Therefore, no *seker* tests were conducted in this school.

TABLE 3.2
Background Characteristics of Study First-Graders by SES and Academic Year (Means, Standard Deviations, and F Values)[a]

	LIP	LP	LI	L	F	MIP	MP	MI	M	F
1973										
Father's education	1.94	2.04	2.00	1.98	.24	4.61	—	4.62	4.46	2.45
	(.54)	(.77)	(.00)	(.52)		(.62)		(.59)	(.76)	
Mother's education	1.96	2.17	2.05	1.95	.72	4.41	—	4.26	4.14	3.50*
	(.71)	(.71)	(.33)	(.67)		(.82)		(.73)	(.94)	
Children in family	3.80	4.94	5.03	5.58	9.18***	2.92	—	2.59	2.50	8.63***
	(1.85)	(2.65)	(2.28)	(2.19)		(1.17)		(1.07)	(.77)	
Father's occupation	1.28	1.21	1.15	1.03	5.09**	2.61	—	2.39	2.51	4.83**
	(.45)	(.47)	(.36)	(.17)		(.62)		(.69)	(.65)	
1974										
Father's education	2.19	2.09	2.06	2.08	.38	4.63	4.64	4.55	4.34	4.82**
	(.40)	(.51)	(.54)	(.52)		(.62)	(.61)	(.58)	(.75)	
Mother's education	2.23	1.97	2.26	2.19	1.45	4.51	4.64	4.30	4.14	6.05***
	(.59)	(.41)	(.85)	(.49)		(.85)	(.61)	(.87)	(.86)	
Children in family	4.27	5.51	4.05	4.92	4.45**	2.78	2.69	3.02	2.55	4.31**
	(1.33)	(2.66)	(1.47)	(2.18)		(1.16)	(.88)	(1.13)	(.91)	
Father's occupation	1.07	1.09	1.28	1.15	2.29	2.59	2.74	2.55	2.30	7.15***
	(.30)	(.28)	(.45)	(.36)		(.63)	(.44)	(.63)	(.73)	

1975

Father's education	2.09	1.57	—	2.10	9.19***	4.43	4.75	—	4.40	2.42
	(.58)	(.63)		(.83)		(.66)	(.64)		(.70)	
Mother's education	2.15	1.45	—	2.09	11.93***	4.18	4.55	—	4.19	1.60
	(.74)	(.70)		(.85)		(1.00)	(.60)		(.80)	
Children in family	4.28	5.22	—	4.80	2.41	2.82	2.85	—	2.64	1.41
	(2.08)	(2.37)		(2.14)		(1.15)	(1.14)		(.99)	
Father's occupation	1.11	1.02	—	1.11	1.74	2.32	2.79	—	2.30	4.22*
	(.31)	(.15)		(.32)		(.69)	(.54)		(.73)	
Mean seker scores (1971-1972)	63.20	62.50	63.09	65.67		82.30	—	77.70[b]	78.30	

[a]Numbers in parentheses are standard deviations.
[b]Estimated mean.
*p < .05
**p < .01
***p < .001

ACHIEVEMENT TESTS

School achievement was measured in two subject areas: arithmetic and reading comprehension. Arithmetic tests were a revised form of the Minkovich New Mathematics Test (1968) for grades 1 and 2. Higher grades were tested with tests developed later on by the Ministry of Education. Reading comprehension was tested by the Ortar and Ben-Shachar (1972) tests which were being developed during the years the research took place.

Standardization of achievement test scores. Discussions about the comparability of group performance over time tend to stress the role of differential growth rates in producing pseudo-effects (Campbell & Boruch, 1975). According to this reasoning higher pretest scores are often indicative of more a rapid growth rate in previous years, leading to an increased gap between a high and a low group in later testing. Covariating for the initial difference between experimental and control groups may lead, under these conditions, to the false conclusion that the treatment has either no effect, or a negative one. Standardization of test scores at each age level is recommended therefore by Campbell and his associates as the best means for eliminating the fan-spread effect caused by these differential growth rates. Following this logic all achievement tests used in the present study were standardized to a mean of 100 and standard deviation of 15 on the research population of each year. This procedure was essential for comparing groups tested at the same time, as well as comparing achievement over time. It should be noted that nation-wide standardized tests were nonexistant in Israel at the time the study was begun.

A comparison of standard scores obtained in the present study with comparable results gathered in a recent nation-wide survey (Minkovich *et al.,* 1977) indicated that, although somewhat different tests were employed, the mean scores and distributions of LC and MC pupils were quite similar.

SELF-IMAGE

Two measures of self-image were used in this study, one an academic self-concept (ASC) measure consisting of two questions requiring the subject to estimate his scores at the end of the year in language and arithmetic. The ASC questions were similar to those used by Brookover and Thomas (1964), while differing from similar measures used by Coleman, Campbell, Hobson, McPartland, Mood, Wernfield, and Tork (1966) and St. John (1971) in at least one important respect. Academic self-concept in the latter studies was a relative measure, that is, the pupil was required to estimate his serial order position in his class.

With the relative method, however, there is at least a theoretical possibility of a serious distortion of the subjects' reported feelings. Suppose, for example, that all the students in one classroom regard themselves as very low achievers, whereas all the students in a second class feel their academic ability to be very high. An absolute measure of ASC will clearly represent these differences, whereas a relative measure may show no difference at all between them. The pupil who is ranked as the last in a very good classroom may estimate his achievement to be at the B level. The psychological meaning of being last may be quite different from occupying the same position while estimating oneself to be a failure. An absolute rather than relative measure of ASC was therefore used in the present study.

A general self-concept measure was also employed (Minkovich et al., 1977, Chapter 8). This part of the study is reported elsewhere (Persitz, 1977) and will not be detailed in what follows.

SOCIOMETRIC MEASURES

Two sociometric questions were used in the present study as a partial measure of social interaction in the various groups tested. Subjects were asked to indicate those classmates with whom they study, and those with whom they play during recess periods.

All tests were group administered during the usual school hours, on the last month of each school year, to all the pupils who were present in their classrooms on the testing day; this was done for each of the successive years (1971–1975). Tests were administered by student assistants trained by the research team rather than by teachers, in order to avoid possible testing biases. Additional data were collected by means of formal and informal observations in the classrooms, and by detailed interviews of students, teachers, principals, and ministry officials.

To recapitulate, the study was constructed so as to approximate a factorial experimental design under actual field conditions. Since such designs presumably control for the major relevant variables, a direct comparison of group means can be made. The design comes close to fulfilling the requirements set down by St. John (1975) as necessary preconditions for an adequate study of integration programs: (1) equivalence of subgroups to be compared in terms of such factors as SES, IQ, age, etc.; (2) equivalence of educational programs in integrated and nonintegrated schools; and (3) continuity of pupil population over the period studied. We have pointed out earlier the places where the data fall short of meeting these demands. However, the present study meets two additional requirements that might be added to St. John's list. First, longitudinal data are gathered to allow for examining within-subject processes. Second, the study of successive cohorts affords the possibility of checking the stability of findings over several groups of subjects, over several points in time.

In studies of such complexity, a common statistical solution is that of some form of multivariate analysis. In our early data analysis, we employed three- and four-way analyses of variance. As discussed by Cronbach (1975), we found that significant interactions, rather than main effects, more often than not were the major outcome. The meaning of significant main effects under such conditions is extremely problematic. It seemed, therefore, more appropriate to use the moderator variable method, dividing the sample into meaningful subgroups and directly comparing pairs of subgroup measures. This makes for greater clarity of both analysis and presentation, and helps differentiate main and interaction effects. This form of analysis is recommended when there is good reason to expect that there are different trends in subgroup performance when divided on the moderator variable. Early results of the present study (Eshel & Klein, 1978) suggested strongly that this was the case, and the method was applied throughout the ensuing analyses.

Longitudinal or Cross-Sectional Research Design?

Most of the available data on the impact of schooling on educational outcomes for children are of an inferential nature. Major issues of behavioral, emotional, or cognitive developmental trends have, with very few exceptions, been investigated by cross-sectional research designs, rather than by direct follow-up of the same group of pupils for several years. The problems of drawing developmental generalization from cross-sectional data have been extensively discussed by various authors (Cook & Campbell, 1976). They raise a major objection to the untested assumption that different cohorts of students are essentially similar to one another despite the differences between them in age, educational environment, and teachers. The low rate of replicability of educational research results (Averch, Carroll, Donaldson, Kiesling, & Pincas, 1975) points at the vulnerability of this assumption, suggesting that both cohort effects and the impact of specific factors such as better teaching or altered motivation should also be taken into account.

The prevalence of the cross-sectional design draws upon two sources representing both pragmatism and basic educational belief: (1) the fact that longitudinal studies are as a rule time-consuming, expensive, and impractical in the existing academic reward system, and (2) the assertion that without assuming a fair amount of consistency over time and subjects, there is no point at all in most types of educational research. If every interaction between pupils, teacher, and their learning environment is unique and noncomparable with other seemingly similar school settings, the only reasonable investigative approach is the case-study. This approach is indeed advocated by Cronbach (1975), although it is not quite clear how generalizations can be drawn.

A major methodological weakness in cross-sectional analysis of the kind presented in our study deserves further discussion: the issue of replication. Scarcity of replications in educational studies, and inconsistent results of partial replications are often described as major obstacles for better understanding classroom processes in relation to educational outcomes (Averch *et al.,* 1975). The present data, based on several consecutive school years, seem to provide a satisfactory answer to this criticism. However, there is substantial overlapping of the various samples. In other words, we are not dealing with independent samples of children as would be required by "true" replication. Two possible methods come to mind in attempting to support the claim that the accumulated findings go beyond the contribution of any single sample. The first involves dividing the total sample into two independent subsamples, as, for instance, comparing the first to third grades in 1971–1973 to similar grades in 1973–1975. The second might be accomplished by splitting the total sample, and then analyzing the two halves separately.

Unfortunately, both methods leave much to be desired. For some reason, some cohorts perform better than others even though no measured differences appear to distinguish among them upon entering school. A cross-sectional comparison may lead to misleading conclusions under these conditions, mistakenly identifying differences among cohorts as a finding of no replication. The split-half method may suffer from the opposite shortcoming. Whenever school atmosphere and policy are important ingredients of academic performance, splitting pupils within the same school almost by necessity raises the probability of a successful replication. This does not necessarily lead to the conclusion that the whole issue should be dropped as insoluble. On the contrary, longitudinal studies seem to provide an answer for some of the problems of the cross-sectional design by limiting the use of inferences on comparability of population and replacing them with intrasubject analyses. The major methodological objection to longitudinal studies is based on practical rather than theoretical reasons, related to the issue of experimental mortality. Children drop out of schools and out of experimental samples representing types of schooling for various reasons. Some of these can be termed random and cause no systematic sampling bias. Other reasons are related more directly to the school, representing both parental attempts to improve their children's education and the schools' efforts to improve their student body (Chen, Kfir, & Fresco, 1975; Coleman et al., 1966). When this is the case, the representativeness of the final sample can be seriously questioned. Existing follow-up studies in desegregated settings suggest that meeting the condition of minimal experimental mortality is indeed a difficult undertaking (Gerard & Miller, 1975).

This study is not an exception in this respect. Only part of our cumulative total of 7000 children actually met the research criteria (see the following section). Three major reasons account for this fact in addition to a process of self-selection initiated by either the schools or the parents: (1) pupil "mortality" in the present study reflects in part changes in sampling throughout the period investigated; (2) since all the existing cohorts in the studied schools were included, there is a considerable number of pupils who were tested for 1 or 2 years only; and (3) a lack of standardized Israeli achievement tests at the outset of the research further decreased the number of pupils with a full test record. A direct test of possible sampling biases caused by the reduced longitudinal sample,

TABLE 3.3
Distribution of Study Sample Cohorts: Type of School, SES, and Grade Level

Cohort	Grade	LIP		LP		LI		L		MIP		MI		M		Totals	
		Arit.	Read	Arit.	Read	Arit.	Read	Arit.	Read	Arit.	Read	Arit.	Read	Arit.	Read	Arit.	Read
1970	3	—	38	—	50	—	—	—	35	—	62	—	—	—	140	—	325
	4	42	39	34	35	6	6	63	64	69	60	14	13	253	171	481	388
	5	38	37	55	53	6	6	49	70	60	64	13	15	247	246	468	491
	6	38	37	38	47	6	6	58	66	60	64	13	13	273	269	486	502
1971	1	58	—	76	—	11	—	—	—	99	—	12	—	—	—	256	—
	2	59	59	74	76	7	—	—	—	103	109	16	—	77	83	336	327
	3	60	59	63	54	27	27	37	42	117	115	52	44	173	121	529	462
	4	41	57	78	72	28	28	37	39	85	114	51	53	173	140	493	503
	5	59	58	70	67	27	24	40	31	119	116	49	50	165	168	529	514
1972	1	48	50	65	65	15	15	—	—	103	96	36	37	78	74	345	337
	2	43	45	67	36	49	52	39	38	91	88	124	124	118	115	531	498
	3	53	40	66	68	51	51	39	36	99	85	126	118	121	75	555	473
	4	48	48	51	62	49	46	41	38	90	92	115	117	113	110	507	513
1973	1	51	45	25	36	72	65	54	55	108	99	148	147	118	116	576	563
	2	50	59	40	38	73	72	56	54	110	111	152	154	115	115	596	597
	3	52	50	38	38	67	67	58	55	100	106	146	149	120	115	581	580

Type of school

47

TABLE 3.4
Analysis of Variance of Background Characteristics: Study Sample Cohorts versus "Dropouts" (F Values)

	LC				MC			
	1970	1971	1972	1973	1970	1971	1972	1973
Father's origin								
Dropout	.22	.58	2.49	.06	1.68	1.13	13.45**	.03
Dropout by type of school	1.93	.59	.10	1.43	.61	1.23	4.18*	3.52*
Mother's origin								
Dropout	.00	.23	.03	.55	1.94	.62	8.30**	8.51**
Dropout by type of school	1.17	1.03	1.01	1.94	1.82	.89	1.98	.58
Father's education								
Dropout	3.64	.45	.27	1.27	2.16	5.35*	1.02	.12
Dropout by type of school	1.04	.31	.94	2.59	.25	.08	.35	1.08
Mother's education								
Dropout	.58	2.68	.46	.37	4.74*	1.43	2.91	1.45
Dropout by type of school	.17	.10	1.96	1.22	1.18	.11	.23	.94
Father's occupation								
Dropout	.36	2.40	.29	.35	2.63	5.93*	1.23	.06
Dropout by type of school	3.43*	.34	.49	1.00	2.44	.78	1.89	2.07
Mother's occupation								
Dropout	.06	.44	.34	.08	.02	.36	4.49*	.74
Dropout by type of school	.96	.63	1.19	1.47	.13	12.93***	.86	.18
Number of children								
Dropout	5.59*	.41	1.69	.38	.28	1.49	2.89	.46
Dropout by type of school	1.65	.86	1.50	1.06	5.32**	4.52*	1.09	1.29

*p < .05.
**p < .01.
***p < .001.

suggesting that representativeness was not seriously violated, is presented later on in this chapter (see Table 3.4).

Rather than choosing arbitrarily between the two methodologies and presenting the data either longitudinally or cross-sectionally, the authors decided to take advantage of both the ability to study trends within pupils over time inherent in the first, and the benefit of the larger samples of the second. Findings in this book are therefore presented both ways.

It was assumed that the follow-up data based on a smaller sample would support and strengthen the cross-sectional analysis depicting the total sample. It was further assumed that despite the differences between the samples, the cohort analysis would essentially replicate the cross-sectional findings. It was also expected that results would show a high level of similarity among consecutive cohorts, and over parallel nonlongitudinal analyses.

Cohort Sample

An examination of the data showed that quite a number of pupils missing in any given year's results did not actually leave their schools, but "reappeared" in following years. The longitudinal sample was therefore defined as all pupils who participated in the study for 3 years or more. Four cohorts in our sample lent themselves to this form of longitudinal analysis (i.e., those beginning school in the years 1970–1973). Later cohorts were not studied long enough to meet the above criterion. Distribution of the longitudinal subsamples is presented in Table 3.3.

It is clear from the table that most of the missing data are accounted for by incomplete information in the first grades, while in later years the numbers tend to be fairly constant over class levels and type of test used. The extent to which the cohort samples are representative of the total sample was determined by comparing background characteristics of pupils included in the longitudinal analysis to those of the "dropouts." Examination of Table 3.4 indicates a small number of significant differences. These inconsistent differences over cohorts and SES origin strongly suggest that no serious sampling bias had taken place.

4

Integration and Achievement

One of the most remarkable aspects of the integration controversy in Israel and the United States has been the assumed association between school integration and improved achievement of minority group pupils. This note was already struck in the 1954 U.S. Supreme Court decision, when the Court's findings were as follows:

> Segregation of white and black children in public schools has a detrimental effect upon the black children. The impact is greater when it has the force of law; for the policy of separating the races is usually interpreted as denoting the inferiority of the Negro group. A sense of inferiority affects the motivation of the child to learn. Segregation with the sanction of law, therefore, has a tendency to retard educational and mental development of Negro children and to deprive them of some of the benefits they would receive in a racial(ly) integrated school system [347 U.S. at 494].

This passage is unique in several ways, not the least of which is the fact that it represented the first time social science data had been used to support a court decision. In an amazingly brief and concise manner, the Court brought problems of social structure, individual

51

psychology, and school achievement into a single context. Moreover, in a series of "if–then" statements, the Court appeared to link these different areas into a causal sequence. Social arrangements, such as the racial composition of schools, mediated by self-perception and motivational effects, are directly involved in cognitive outcomes for minority children. As written, the sense of this causal sequence is primarily negative (i.e., it speaks of *detrimental* effects under segregated conditions, and says nothing about outcomes under integrated conditions). However, the implication of such a causal linkage is clear: School integration should reverse the situation and help bring about improved minority achievement.

Thus, 12 years before the first major study to test this proposition was carried out, a powerful association between integration and achievement had already been created. It carried both the force of law and a strong humanitarian appeal, as well as a rather uncomplicated approach to the solution of a major educational problem. The presence of a middle term—the mediating effects of self-perception on motivation—suggested that there was no necessary one-to-one correlation between changes in the schools and educational outcomes. However, this middle term could easily be taken to be a psychological by-product of certain structural manipulations, and therefore a reinforcement of the simplicity of the basic premise. Interestingly, much of the later psychological theorizing about the effects of integration closely adhered to the lines first laid down by the Court. Gerard and Miller (1975), for example, have summarized many of the social science assumptions underlying school desegregation policy. All the hypotheses they mentioned focus on presumed changes in the minority child as a result of *exposure* to the integrated school situation in which there is a white majority. The various investigations of school integration, beginning with the 1966 EEOS study (Coleman *et al.*, 1966), also implicitly accepted the approach outlined by the Court. The debate over the results of these studies is still very much alive today, and still concerned with trying to demonstrate the correctness or incorrectness of the original assumptions (Cook, 1979; Stephan, 1978).

Social scientists have not been able to agree on either the impact of integrated education on achievement or on other key issues, such as the nature of the self-image resulting from intergroup interaction. Reviewing most of the existing literature, St. John (1975) concluded that in certain cases integration was associated with improved achievement, self-concept, and social standing of the minority pupil; in other instances it had no significant effect; and in a few, negative effects following integration were noted (see also Crain & Mahard, 1978). Recent studies in Israel (Chen, Lewy, & Kfir, 1977; Minkovich *et al.*, 1977) have also questioned whether integration as such has any effect on the academic achievement of the less advanced group in the classroom.

All the controversy, however, has not diminished the power and continuing influence of the original idea. In the United States, the association of the integration–achievement link with a constitutional issue, and thus with major questions of law, morality and justice, has helped create an imperative that it somehow *must* work (one writer suggesting that researchers concentrate on providing results and findings that can be used as tools in the creation and strengthening of an egalitarian social movement [Woock, 1977].) Furthermore, the very simplicity of the formulation has made it highly attractive both politically and administratively when dealing with problems of minority groups. The recent history of programs for the disadvantaged can offer many examples of efforts to devise one or another educational intervention with the promise of relatively quick and effective results. And finally, the causal sequence as formulated by the Court and expanded on by others is a bold expression of a classic liberal ideal: A dedicated rearrangement of social and institutional forces can undo the effects of past evils and lead to the betterment of all.

Israel offers many parallels to the ideas just noted, but also some important differences. As far as its own "disadvantaged" population is concerned, Israel presents no long history of pain, violence, and discrimination, legalized or otherwise. Calling for integration of different elements of Israeli society has not been seen primarily as an issue of correcting an historical or social wrong. Instead, it is a way of reaffirming a cardinal value upon which the State was founded—that of *mizug galuyot*, or, literally, the "intermingling of the exiles." This is a principle with a number of different meanings. Most prominent among them, on the one hand, is the blending of Jews of many different backgrounds into a cohesive and distinct national entity. On the other is the uplifting of culturally backward elements to a level necessary for full participation in a technically and socially advanced society. The need for reaffirmation of this principle under the heading of integration in recent years seems to stem from a troubled appreciation of the fact that the "intermingling" process has been achieved only in part. Whether from neglect or growing privatization, lack of imagination or any of many other reasons that have been offered, large sections of the Israeli population—generally identified as those of Asian-African origin—are behind economically, socially, and educationally. Awareness of this situation creates peculiar tensions in, as a leading Israeli sociologist has characterized the country, "a relatively small modern society, but one possessed of aspirations toward a wider, greater social and cultural standing [Eisenstadt, 1977, p. 6]."

The pressure for rapid acculturation and structural assimilation of many different immigrant groups makes for even greater salience of the integration–achievement association. In 1969, the Israeli parliament decided upon an educational reform which would radically reorganize post-elementary education and create a new system of comprehensive high schools. The intent of the reform was stated quite clearly:

> The program of educational reform at the junior high school level aims jointly at two central goals: a) raising and strengthening the educational level; and b) speeding up the process of social integration among various cultural and social groups [Chen, Lewy, & Adler, 1978, p. 9].

In the debate centering around the reform, the possibility of narrowing the achievement gap between different groups in Israeli society through integrated education was almost a foregone conclusion. No particular theory was offered in justification; if anything, the link was taken to be self-evident, the emphasis instead on the contribution of such a linkage to more rapidly attaining national ideals. An additional indication of both the primacy of these ideals (uncodified, since Israel does not as yet have a constitution) and the presumed connection between integration and achievement can be found in the few Israeli court decisions around cases stemming from parental opposition to the Educational Reform program. Responding to the claim of middle-class European parents that they had the right to send their children to whichever school they wished (meaning select, middle-class institutions), the Israeli Supreme Court, sitting as the High Court of Justice, ruled against the parents, and explicitly cited the aims of the Reform program in justification.

In the absence of a national constitution, as Goldstein (in press) points out, the major role of the Israeli Supreme Court has been to protect the individual against the encroachment of excessive government control. It is, therefore, all the more striking that on this issue the Court chose to reaffirm the collective goal of integration. On this issue, the Court set aside claims of individual free choice, while accepting as both fact and justification the association of integration and achievement.

In spite of equivocal research data, it would seem that a belief in the impact of integration on achievement has important social uses, some of which have already been mentioned. Still, the fact that researchers have been unable to arrive at a consistent answer is not altogether surprising. Most of the research in the field has followed the basic paradigm of examining the relation of classroom social structure to learning outcomes. It is quite plausible, however, that other variables related to, or part of, the integrated setting may explain some of the inconsistencies in current research. School en-environment, teacher quality, teaching methods, curricula, interpersonal relations among pupils, or teacher attitudes, are a few of the possible explanatory mechanisms suggested in the literature. The need for a different kind of research stressing situational variables of a similar nature has now been recognized by several observers (Cook, 1979; Schofield, 1978; Stephan, 1978; St. John, 1975.) However, very few studies have so far examined, much less systematically manipulated, social or learning processes in integrated settings (Aronson *et al.,* 1978; Gerard & Miller, 1975; Sharan, 1980).

On the other hand, the situation in Israel offers an interesting possibility for re-examining the basic paradigm. Conceivably, the simple causal sequence discussed above has a better chance of operating where intergroup tensions are not high, where deeply irrational elements such as racial feelings are not prominent, where there is no history of legalized discrimination to overcome, and where emphasis on achievement for all is a major feature of the educational system. All of those elements should form a more effective context for the mediating effects of intergroup contact to take place. Examining the direct impact of integration in Israel may, therefore, provide a way of asking whether or not the presumed cognitive outcomes are a culturally or socially specific phenomenon, or if there are general and more universal processes involved.

In this chapter, the findings on school achievement for over 7000 elementary school children are presented, many of whom were retested for anywhere from 2 to 5 consecutive years. As detailed in

Chapter 3, not all children included when the study was begun were tested in subsequent years, and the data on children included in later phases of the study are necessarily limited. We will examine the stability of various findings over the years in which the study took place. This will be done cross-sectionally as well as by an analysis of longitudinal trends for specific subgroups.

Results

CROSS-SECTIONAL ANALYSIS

Mean performance scores for integrated and nonintegrated children in schools not employing the activity method are presented in Figures 4.1 and 4.2. Examination of the means of the two LC groups (L and LI) does not seem to indicate any consistently large differences between them for any of the study years. Two-way analyses of variance were used to examine the effects of integration and grade level separately for each of the follow-up years. No significant effect of integration on reading scores is indicated in the 3 years presented in Table 4.1. In only 1 out of 3 consecutive years is there a significant effect of integration on arithmetic achievement (Table 4.1).

Further analysis shows that LI classes outperformed comparable L groups on 9 out of 14 comparisons in reading comprehension (Figure 4.2), and on 11 out of 14 comparisons on arithmetic (see Figure 4.1). Sign tests applied to these figures suggest the overall differences between the groups on both tests to be significant at the .05 level.

The few interaction effects found in the analysis of variance do not, however, signify any clear-cut trend over years in school. Instead, they seem to represent random fluctuations or specific effects other than those that might be referable to the impact of integration (Figures 4.1 and 4.2). Although there is some marginal advantage for the integrated groups, the data lend no clear support to the contention that integration as such made a meaningful contribution toward ameliorating the academic performance of LC pupils. This finding closely parallels that for Israeli MC and LC junior high schools pupils in integrated settings as found in a recent major study (Chen *et al.*, 1978).

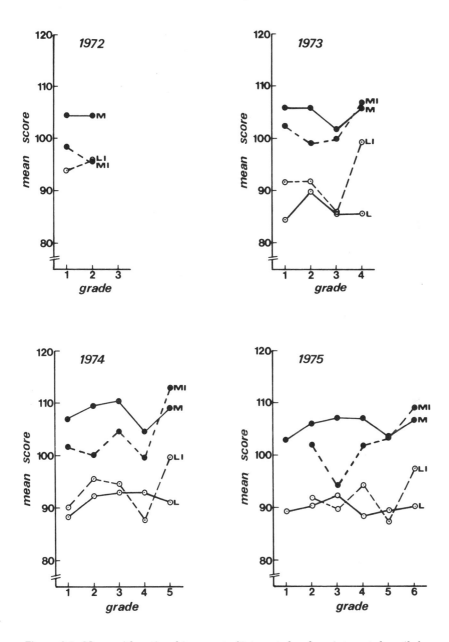

Figure 4.1. Mean arithmetic achievement of integrated and nonintegrated pupils by academic year, grade level, and type of school.

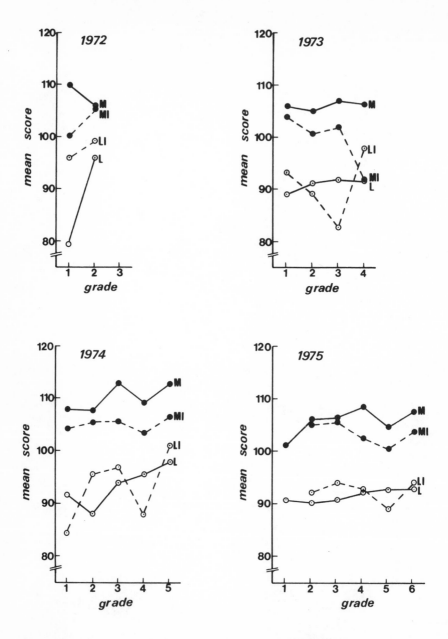

Figure 4.2. Mean reading comprehension achievement of integrated and nonintegrated pupils by academic year, grade level, and type of school.

TABLE 4.1
Analysis of Variance of Academic Achievement of Integrated and Nonintegrated Pupils

	1972			1973			1974			1975		
	MS	df	F	MS	df	F	MS	df	F	MS	df	F
ARITHMETIC												
LC												
Grade level				279.89	3	1.87	406.43	4	2.20	83.16	4	.44
Integration				1940.61	1	12.98***	446.43	1	2.41	244.49	1	1.30
Interaction				428.37	3	2.87*	326.92	4	1.77	518.26	4	2.76*
Residual				149.51	402		185.05	562		187.86	685	
MC												
Grade level	66.22	1	.41	1280.14	3	8.02***	1506.41	4	9.50***	828.39	4	5.53***
Integration	4943.96	1	30.63***	4180.02	1	26.17***	7728.11	1	48.72***	9405.55	1	62.76***
Interaction	113.82	1	.71	545.80	3	3.42*	669.04	4	4.22**	1760.24	4	11.75***
Residual	161.44	467		159.71	1477		158.61	1371		149.87	1358	
READING COMPREHENSION												
LC												
Grade level	1247.74	1	7.23**	220.86	3	1.20	1257.44	4	6.89***	97.88	4	.48
Integration	5890.15	1	34.15***	14.13	1	.08	292.97	1	1.61	195.41	1	.96
Interaction	2466.96	1	14.30***	857.40	3	4.67**	1171.11	4	6.42***	145.87	4	.71
Residual	172.48	199		183.81	404		182.48	590		204.58	606	
MC												
Grade level	574.69	1	5.09*	252.28	3	1.45	835.36	4	5.17***	415.57	4	.48
Integration	7657.44	1	67.80***	4762.36	1	27.38***	5207.85	1	32.23***	2635.25	1	16.89***
Interaction	302.28	1	2.68	642.07	3	3.69*	247.23	4	1.53	302.00	4	1.94
Residual	112.94	566		173.94	1328		161.60	1278		156.06	1359	

*p < .05
**p < .01
***p < .001

Similar computations carried out separately for the MC data present a somewhat different pattern. As can be seen from Figure 4.1, the arithmetic performance of nonintegrated pupils (M) surpassed that of their integrated peers (MI) during the first years at school. What seems to be a movement toward closing the gap in the higher grades actually represents higher achievement scores of a single, more successful cohort (the children in fourth grade in 1973). Examination of Figure 4.2 suggests a rather similar picture: Pupils in M groups show some advantage over MI pupils in each of the pairs presented. The mean difference between the groups is approximately 4 points. Table 4.1 indicates these differences to be significant at the .001 level in each of the years represented in the figures.

LONGITUDINAL ANALYSIS

Examination of the performance of specific cohorts of L and LI pupils over time strengthens the conclusion derived from the cross-sectional analyses (see Tables 4.2 and 4.3). In seven out of eight longitudinal comparisons, there were no significant average differences over years in school between L and LI pupils in either arithmetic or reading comprehension. This suggests that the occasional significant differences found in the cross-sectional data do not reflect the effect of integration upon performance, but indicate variations in base-level achievement among the cohorts. As far as the performance of almost any specific cohort is concerned, however, there was no discriminable main effect of integration upon the achievement of LC pupils.

In three out of the four analyses of arithmetic achievement, a significant grade effect was found for LC pupils. Examination of the means suggests that it was mainly the improved performance of the L subgroups over years in school that contributed to this rise. In other words, whatever differences in performance between L and LI subgroups were noted tended to fade over time. Statistically, this trend is significant in two out of the four analyses for arithmetic achievement. No such pattern was found in the data for reading comprehension.

As in the cross-sectional analysis, M pupils almost always scored somewhat higher than their MI peers. However, trend analysis showed that these differences are significant in two out of the four comparisons in reading achievement and in arithmetic

TABLE 4.2
Mean Academic Achievement of Cohort Samples by Integration, Grade Level, and SES

	Cohorts													
	1970			1971				1972				1973		
	Grade 4	Grade 5	Grade 6	Grade 2	Grade 3	Grade 4	Grade 5	Grade 1	Grade 2	Grade 3	Grade 4	Grade 1	Grade 2	Grade 3
ARITHMETIC														
MC														
Integrated	105.3	110.8	109.4	100.8	100.0	102.2	104.7	97.9	99.2	105.2	102.7	102.3	100.8	93.7
Nonintegrated	106.4	109.2	107.0	106.2	99.3	104.5	103.1	105.5	109.1	110.5	107.5	106.0	110.2	107.8
LC														
Integrated	97.0	100.3	97.7	89.3	86.6	88.6	89.5	95.2	93.4	96.9	95.1	92.8	96.8	90.6
Nonintegrated	86.7	91.8	95.5	—	86.3	92.1	98.0	—	91.1	96.9	95.1	86.4	92.6	95.4
READING COMPREHENSION														
MC														
Integrated	90.7	106.1	105.1	107.4	106.4	105.4	102.9	100.8	101.1	106.1	104.0	104.3	105.8	106.2
Nonintegrated	105.6	113.6	107.9	—	102.5	109.4	105.4	111.4	106.7	113.1	109.3	104.8	107.8	106.9
LC														
Integrated	93.9	96.5	93.1	—	83.3	87.3	89.1	97.6	91.3	97.9	94.3	94.2	96.4	95.3
Nonintegrated	92.1	98.2	93.5	—	92.1	95.1	93.9	—	91.5	99.9	96.5	90.3	89.6	92.6

TABLE 4.3
Trend Analysis of Academic Achievement of Cohort Samples (Linear Effects Only)[a]

		Cohorts						
	1970		1971		1972		1973	
	Hyp.MS	$F_{(1.37)}$	Hyp.MS	$F_{(1.54)}$	Hyp.MS	$F_{(1.80)}$	Hyp.MS	$F_{(1.113)}$
ARITHMETIC								
LI versus L								
Grade	701.01	9.91**	1523.97	12.92***	134.52	2.48	454.26	5.63*
Group	296.88	2.65	256.27	1.95	17.61	.15	177.30	1.92
Interaction	70.71	1.40	528.14	4.48*	.89	.02	1822.69	22.59***
	Hyp.MS	$F_{(1.209)}$	Hyp.MS	$F_{(1.72)}$	Hyp.MS	$F_{(1.91)}$	Hyp.MS	$F_{(1.234)}$
MI versus M								
Grade	304.00	4.94*	1.26	.03	302.43	5.59*	1732.58	24.02***
Group	.92	.01	37.06	.52	1020.82	7.88**	4482.55	40.30***
Interaction	211.54	3.44	402.74	24.45***	59.39	1.10	2751.90	38.16***

| | Cohorts | | | | | | | |
| | 1970 | | 1971 | | 1972 | | 1973 | |
	Hyp.MS	F(1.61)	Hyp.MS	F(1.49)	Hyp.MS	F(1.71)	Hyp.MS	F(1.101)
READING COMPREHENSION								
LI versus L								
Grade	259.12	5.18*	140.72	3.94	67.78	1.32	53.18	1.12
Group	48.12	.40	460.24	3.91	.83	.01	645.12	4.70*
Interaction	45.15	.90	211.50	5.92*	6.79	.13	5.60	.12

	Hyp.MS	F(1.137)	Hyp.MS	F(1.115)	Hyp.MS	F(1.65)	Hyp.MS	F(1.232)
MI versus M								
Grade	689.09	10.35**	175.08	3.43	32.32	.65	469.91	10.86**
Group	727.32	5.03*	327.49	2.90	1012.84	8.02**	119.79	1.03
Interaction	625.39	9.40**	51.09	1.56	450.20	9.04**	11.69	.27

[a]ANOVA, trend analysis, SPSS, version 7.0, 1978.

*$p < .05$
**$p < .01$
***$p < .001$

63

when averaged over time. Moreover, in three out of the eight possible comparisons, a significant trend of diminishing differences between MI and M over time was found.

When the data of M and MI subgroups are combined, a generally negatively accelerating pattern is obtained (in six out of eight
comparisons, a significant quadratic effect was found).

Discussion

The schools that were integrated during the course of the present study were, by all available measures (see Chapter 3), among
the best in Jerusalem. Additional confirmation of their status can be
found in Minkovich *et al.*, (1977) who, in 1972–1973, carried out a
broad survey of elementary school education in Israel. These authors found that schools with fewer than 25% disadvantaged children (the situation in the receiving schools in the present study
prior to integration) were consistently superior to all other schools
in the country on a wide variety of measures, including financial
resources, audio-visual equipment, extra-curricular programming,
educational background of staff, and provision of special personnel.
The percentage of LC children admitted into the receiving schools
and represented in all classrooms never exceeded 50%, and was
often lower. No instance of "reverse integration," that is, moving
MC children into schools with a majority of disadvantaged children,
was included in the study sample. The process of integration itself
was carried out in relatively smooth fashion, with no major outbursts, no parent strikes, no overt signs of discontent or disruption.
In other words, the study sample afforded a set of structurally near
optimal circumstances for examining the proposition that the integrated setting can form an educational context in which no children
lose, and one special group of children—the disadvantaged—stands
to gain. Since the EEOS study of 1966 (Coleman *et al.*, 1966), this
proposition has been a major focus of research activity, and, despite
numerous methodological and theoretical critiques, remains an
issue at the heart of much of the debate around integration.

There were enough shortcomings in the design of the present
study to suggest a note of caution about interpretation. As detailed
before (see Chapter 3), there were no pre-tests available prior to the
children's entry into school. Even though no consistent differences

were found among the various subgroups on different background measures (Tables 3.2 and 3.4) the possibility of some selective factor untapped by any of the measures cannot be ruled out. The operation of such a factor may have been added to by the fact that a truly random distribution of children among schools was not carried out. The study relied heavily on an assumption of cultural and social homogeneity of the LC population, and similarity among the various types of schools included. Both of these variables are highly complex and multidimensional, and there are many warnings in the literature about any simple approximation of either of them.

The consistency of results in the present study, however, both over years in school and for different groups of entering children, suggests that we are not dealing with some artifact of design. Integration as such (i.e., including select proportions of LC children into MC high-status schools *with little or no additional form of educational intervention*) had no consistently detectable effect on the achievement of the LC children. This might be stated more positively, for example, that children in integrated schools appeared neither to gain nor to lose educationally. But this is justification of a different order than that generally implied in the debate around the relation of integration to achievement. Moreover, since the results are confined to the elementary school grades, and to a relatively narrow sampling of achievement, there is no way of knowing what this neutral picture of no gains and no losses may mean for the future development and learning of the children involved. The fact that MC children in integrated schools appeared to perform somewhat below expectation raises some very special educational and policy problems that must be carefully examined.

The findings of the present study are in agreement with those of other recently published works, both in Israel and America (Chen *et al.*, 1977; Gerard & Miller, 1975; Minkovich *et al.*, 1977; Patchen, Hofmann, & Brown, 1980), which do not support any causal association between integration and achievement. If there is any difference in the present study, it is the carrying out of a set of near optimal conditions for implementing integration within a close approximation of an experimental framework. The gain in methodological care, however, essentially does not change what must be increasingly clear: The claim for any direct impact on achievement of LC pupils by a political and administrative act of social restructuring in the schools is, perhaps, of ideological importance, but is factu-

ally unfounded. The simple causal sequence embodied in court decisions and legislative acts may represent important beliefs, and may
be necessary for motivating action where difficult-to-achieve programs are concerned. It may even form some partial theoretical base
for guaranteeing the minimal conditions necessary for the expected
association with achievement to take place (see Chapter 5). As it
stands, however, the simple causal sequence, when translated into
an actual program, is more an element of a political strategy that
paradoxically may, at times, help create a situation inimicable to
the effects on achievement toward which it aims. A closer examination of what actually took place in Jerusalem schools undergoing
integration may help illustrate this point.

Elementary school integration as represented in this study
might best be characterized as a principle without a program. School
officials, both in the Ministry of Education and Jerusalem Municipality, were primarily concerned with finding an efficient solution
to many different community pressures. Principles had to be enun-
ciated, formulas devised, and promises made that, in keeping with
the typical style of Israeli political life (see Chapter 3), would
minimize criticism and debate and appear to resolve conflicts by
extending benefits to the largest possible numbers. This is a type of
bureaucratic response which is usually quite effective in providing
immediate short-term solutions to certain issues. It allows for public
commitment to ideals in the broadest possible perspective, while, for
the most part, screening a reluctance or organizational inability to
face up to the many complex problems that may stem from the
decision. This is also an approach which tends to compartmentalize
issues, so that "talking" integration, and its presumed association
with achievement, forced into the background any detailed consideration of special compensatory activities for the disadvantaged
children to be transferred (itself a subject associated with an earlier
and now to be rejected solution).

Furthermore, integration on the elementary school level had
neither the force of law nor the organizational commitment behind
it that the junior high school reorganization had (see Chapter 3, note
7). This meant that each school to be integrated represented an
almost independent problem, to be solved quickly in whatever way
possible, with the school then left to cope as best it could with the
newly created situation. The net effect of all these factors was a
peculiar condition: a public stand affirming the importance of inte-

gration while, as Minkovich *et al.*, (1977) summarized it, "it appears that neither the Ministry of Education, the municipalities nor the parents consider [elementary school] integration to be a special educational enterprise warranting support and special aid [p. 362]." This may sound somewhat strange considering the fact that a major purpose of the present study was to examine a parallel set of integrated schools in Jerusalem to which very special care and attention were given (see Chapter 5). However, as outlined in Chapter 3, these project schools were from the outset considered an isolated experiment—if anything, an exception to prove the general rule.

The centralized and hierarchically structured school system in Israel left little opportunity for the receiving schools themselves to take part in the planning for the integration program. Principals and teachers are near the bottom of the bureaucratic ladder. They were rarely called in for consultation, and whatever fears, doubts, or hesitations they might have voiced were usually interpreted as obstructionist tactics to be overridden as quickly as possible. For example, several receiving school principals were greatly concerned over the reputations of their schools—in at least one instance a reputation for excellence that had been carefully built up over many years and of which the staff were very proud. Given the political rhetoric generated around the subject of integration, however, such anxieties were either disregarded or forcefully put down through various kinds of pressure. Little attention was paid to the possibility that principals and teachers were truly worried about how they themselves would function in the integrated setting. In private conversations with the research team, a number of teachers spoke of the threat that integration posed to their own feelings of professional competence, a threat made all the more salient by the fact that the educational authorities were inordinately silent about what should actually be done in the newly integrated classrooms, once constituted. An interesting confirmation of the conflicting situation in which the teachers found themselves was reported by Minkovich *et al.* (1977) in their survey. A striking majority of the national sample of elementary school teachers in the latter study expressed positive opinions about integrated education. At least half of them, however, felt that "school integration might fail because of the teachers' inability to adapt their teaching methods to heterogeneous classes [p. 361]."

What appears, therefore, as "optimal" conditions for integration, upon closer examination can be found to be seriously problematic. Teachers and principals experienced the integration process as strong pressure to accommodate themselves to a new situation for which there were few operative guidelines, and even fewer sources of guidance and help. Concerned with their abilities as educators, they found that their questioning and criticisms were often taken to be discriminatory and obstructionist. They quickly dropped any public objections, their silence taken as acquiescence and adding to the impression that a smooth and effective transition was taking place in the schools. Left to rely mainly on their own ingenuity and initiative, they often fell back (see what follows) on methods and techniques that tended to reinstate many features of segregated education. Little wonder, then, that the Minkovich survey found that principals and teachers in integrated schools, as compared to all other types of elementary schools, expressed the highest degree of dissatisfaction with their work. The issues raised in this discussion also shed some light on the lack of impact of integration on achievement, even in a situation considered by many to be "optimal."

Whereas there was no noticeable effect of integration on LC pupils' achievement, integrated MC children appeared to have some difficulty, at least in their first few years of school. Of course, the newly integrated classroom presented the teacher with a major dilemma: how to divide one's time and whom to teach? Many field observations suggest that teachers, confronted by a heterogeneous classroom, will tend to work with the brighter children and pay less attention to the others (Rist, 1970, 1978).

If this were the case, then it is all the more surprising that it was the usually higher-achieving MC pupils in integrated classrooms whose academic performance was slightly less than might be expected. A plausible avenue of interpretation requires some additional information about the Israeli elementary school.

The first few grades of school in Israel, as is probably the case in many other countries, focus very heavily on basics. Children are expected to be able to read halfway through the first year; the four arithmetical operations for numbers less than 100 should be acquired by the second year, and so on. While a great deal of content is offered, the pace, in terms of conceptual increments, is relatively unpressured during the early years. Toward the end of the third year, and particularly in the fourth grade, however, there is a noticeable increase in demands of the standard curriculum for all Israeli schools. New subject matter is rapidly introduced, the number of separate subjects covered increases, and there is generally an atmosphere of a race against time as teachers try to cover everything the curriculum demands by the end of elementary school. (The congestion of the elementary school curriculum in Israel has been subjected to over 20 years of criticism [Adar, 1956; Kleinberger, 1969; Minkovich *et al.*, 1977] but has yet to undergo any thorough analysis or structural revision.) These are also the grades where ability grouping is first employed in the effort both to meet curriculum demands and to offer help to those who are by now seriously falling behind. In this respect, it is important to note that Minkovich found that the most extensive use of ability grouping was made in those Israeli schools defined as "integrated."

Given this background, we can suggest that the following process might be involved in the achievement profile of the MI children in our sample. Teachers in newly integrated classrooms must find ways of moving all the children to some minimally acceptable level of achievement. This level, however, both individually and collectively, must be continually readjusted and negotiated in light of successes and failures, time, energy, expectations, and possibilities of support. In the absence of any particular guidelines, techniques, or structure for working with the class, the teachers will probably divide their attention and/or continually alter the learning pace in such a way as to provide the MC children with inconsistent attention, standard setting, and reward. This inconsistency, coupled with what teachers have described as "organizational problems" in the early grades of the integrated school, may have an effect on the motivation or cognitive intake, or both, of the MC children.

In the upper grades, the increased use of organizational aids such as ability grouping means that, for many subjects, the MC children will be together in a group of their own. Their teachers can now concentrate on their level alone, and there is no longer any pressure to compromise with the learning pace of others. However, schools tend to structure and maintain performance expectations that are set quite early in the child's school career. The results of earlier performance may then be passed on and institutionalized, not only for LC children—a finding that has been well documented —but for MC children as well.

If the interpretation just presented is anywhere near correct, it raises the troubling possibility that without some form of pedagogical adjustment integration may sometimes have a constricting effect on the achievement of MC children. Although occasional "spontaneous" recovery from such constriction was found in our data, there was no clear-cut way to account for it. Such effects do not necessarily mean that the MC child in the integrated school will have his cognitive abilities impaired, or that something detrimental to his achievement will "rub off" through association with his LC classmates. Instead, the stress placed on some variant of a "lateral transmission of values" theory in accounting for MC and LC pupil performance has obscured elements of the actual classroom process. The key issue may be more a matter of what is expected and demanded of the child by teachers who must solve the complex problem of dealing with and setting standards for many different children, with only limited techniques and concepts for how to accomplish this. The problem is that most of the research that has dealt with the impact of integration on the achievement of MC children contains hardly any reference to what takes place, educationally or otherwise, in the classroom. It may be, in fact, that the discrepancies in existing research—some demonstrating a detrimental effect and some not—are at least in part due to different kinds of internal school adjustments which go unnoticed in the data analysis. This means that the results of different studies would hardly be comparable, and underlines the need for more detailed and specific case study material in future research. The question will eventually have to be asked: What *types* of classroom arrangements and interventions are associated with positive, negative, or no changes in the achievement of one or both groups in the integrated classroom?

At least some of the possible internal classroom adjustments, such as those involving teacher attitudes, peer acceptance, and grade normalization, have begun to be examined (Gerard & Miller, 1975). Other possibilities ranging from special compensatory activities to programs of active parent involvement have been suggested by various authors (Cook, 1979; Forehand & Ragosta, 1976; Miller, 1977; Orfield, 1975; Pettigrew *et al.*, 1976; St. John, 1975), but often appear contradictory when placed side by side and "shown to be based more on personal ideology, strands of theory, and hunches than on any consistent and clearly developed theoretical or empirical perspective [Porter, 1976]."

All of these authors agree, however, on one point which is supported by the data presented in this chapter. Without some additional form of intervention, there is no reason to expect that the physical rearrangement of classroom populations has a necessary connection with changes in achievement. The "best" possible conditions for integration, usually defined in terms of classroom percentage formulas, status of receiving schools, lack of intergroup tension, and so on, and embodied in the causal sequence described at the outset of this chapter, perhaps reflect a political and administrative definition of "success." There is no automatic guarantee, however, that the promise of improved achievement for one part of the population, and at least no change for another, can be used as justification for carrying out such measures. To do so, in the absence of any serious consideration for what happens in the classroom, is truly to convert the schools into a political and ideological instrument, and thus to carry out ends which, some critics feel, have no place in the schools (Frankenstein, 1976; Kleinberger, 1973; Lamm, 1974).

Furthermore, as we tried to illustrate in the discussion of how the Jerusalem schools responded to the decision to integrate, the pressures and bureaucratic forms of the political process may help create a situation in which little attention is paid to how the program will work educationally—where even asking such questions may be taken as signs of defeatism and defensiveness. Left to themselves, the schools may or may not then hit upon some way to deal with the new situation. In our own data, this seems to have resulted in little benefit for the LC children, and the suggestion of some constricting effect on the achievement of MC pupils. What cannot be overlooked however, is the fact that the differences noted in both groups were, in absolute terms, extremely small. Even though the MI group, for example, was lower in achievement, this was mostly a matter of mean difference of 3 or 4 test points, enough to reach statistical significance, but not necessarily indicative of major educational importance. All the MC children were achieving well above their LC classmates and within the same general range—in a sense, an additional confirmation of the stability of school impact even in the case of organizational change.

The findings presented in this chapter underline the problem of trying to base policy decisions on research which deals in only the simplest outline form with inputs and outcomes, and where some of the potentially most significant variables remain unknown. In this light, nothing of what has been presented in this chapter can allow for any sort of conclusion as to whether or not integration "works." What we have done so far is to assess a set of conditions under which integration and school achievement remain more or less unrelated. In the following chapter we turn to another set of conditions, and a different kind of outcome.

5

Integration, Open Education, and Academic Performance

For the teacher facing an integrated classroom, its most immediate and problematic aspect is the wide, sometimes extreme, range of abilities it contains. The planners of the experimental project felt that any educational solution to this problem that accepted the challenge of maintaining classroom integrity (i.e., not resorting to various forms of resegregation) needed to incorporate some variant of individualized learning and instruction. Both structurally and pedagogically, traditional classroom practice had to be sufficiently modified so that—simply put—the brighter pupil would, when necessary, advance at his own pace without being bored by waiting for the slower pupils to catch up, whereas the slower pupil would have the chance to master basic material without the frustration of always comparing himself or herself unfavorably with others. A revision had to be found that would help extricate the teacher from the terrible bind of having to choose how to allocate his or her time so that some particular subgroup of pupils would not suffer.

As outlined in Chapter 3, the approach chosen for introduction into the project schools was that of the activity classroom. This was a form of open education that had up until then been experimentally tried out in a few Israeli preschool settings. In a surprisingly short period of time, the activity method in the project schools changed from an auxiliary device designed to help manage certain features of the heterogeneous classroom into an educational issue whose popularity almost threatened to overshadow other, no less important, aspects of the project. The activity method rapidly became highly fashionable in Israeli elementary education, so that within a few years, hundreds of classrooms all over the country began shifting to activity methods and techniques. An examination of the activity classes in the project as defined by observational measures is presented in Chapter 9. The following description, however, given by teachers who practiced the method, conveys a general impression that may help clarify issues to be touched upon in the research findings.

> The activity method is based upon the individual work of the pupil in accord with his own activity, motivation, pace, and interests. In order to implement these principles, the classroom is equipped with various "work corners" to which the child can be attracted in keeping with his interests. Every such corner contains graded materials at various levels of difficulty. The arithmetic corner, for example, contains exercises, learning games, and problems, as well as stories and other materials. . . . The child's activity is guided by the teacher, rather than being imposed or forced. Classroom organization, rather than imposed rules or regulations, creates the opportunity for the child to utilize almost all the work corners at various times. (These corners include: clay modeling, drawing, sewing, carpentry, natural science, reading, drama, etc.) . . . The teacher guides the pupils in developing observational skills. For instance, pupils were encouraged to keep a diary of observations on the development of a new child in the family, or the construction of a new building nearby the child's home. With the teacher's help, pupils learned to note, follow and organize changes; to see similarities among different phenomena, and variety in similar events; to analyze events into their component parts, and to see the whole as something beyond a collection of elements. . . .
>
> The activity method creates and facilitates opportunities for small-group encounters among children in order to carry out specific tasks. In the context of small groups, children talk and listen to one another, sometimes in what appears to be complete disorder. However, different opinions are constantly emerging and choices must be made. Each participant must bring forward reasons powerful enough to convince others, analyze alternatives, and choose what in his opinion, seems to be best. All the pupils experience the need for group process in diagnosing and deciding upon methods of implementation. . . . Different assignments may call for dif-

ferent group composition. Each new task is an experience that requires consideration of new variables and the characteristics of group members. Since the focus is on a real task, involvement is generally high . . . [Israel Ministry of Education and Culture, 1973, 1978].

We have already pointed out (Chapter 3) how a combination of public relations on the part of the school administration, feelings of challenge and satisfaction shared by teachers, and reduced antagonism and resistance among the middle-class parents helped promote a general belief in the success of the project. This success became common knowledge even before the initial results of the follow-up study were collected and analyzed.

The project schools rapidly began to attract growing numbers of visits from interested teachers and Ministry officials, as well as university experts. The obvious motivation and excitement of both teachers and pupils, standing in striking contrast to the traditional Israeli classroom, conveyed a refreshing feeling of both change and accomplishment. A large measure of this initial enthusiasm can probably be linked to the simple fact of change, as well as to some features generally thought to be characteristic of the open educational setting. The latter is regarded by many educators as an optimistic fulfillment of long-held aspirations: Children learning in open schools are described as lively, open-minded, independent, and creative by both teachers and outside observers (Silberman, 1973; Weber, 1971). Research findings, however, tend to be more reserved, and indicate inconsistent relationships between open education and many different educational outcomes (McPartland & Epstein, 1977; Traub, Weiss, & Fisher, 1974). Moreover, the specific usefulness of the activity method as a way of solving learning problems of the disadvantaged child has been seriously questioned. Results of various studies have ranged from findings of no effects on achievement (Foreman & McKinney, 1978; Ward & Barcher, 1975; Wright, 1975), to an actual lowering of test scores (Evans, 1979; Traub, Weiss, Fisher, & Musella, 1972). A recent review of 102 studies indicates 14 favoring open schools, 12 favoring traditional schools, 19 with mixed results, and 47 with no significant differences (Horowitz, 1970).

The discrepancy between practitioner enthusiasm and research results is an interesting problem in itself, but cannot be taken as definitive. Many of the studies involving the effects of integration and educational intervention on the disadvantaged child are beset with major methodological difficulties that seriously limit the conclusions that can be drawn (St. John, 1975; Stephan, 1978). Specific features of the context in which special methods such as activity classrooms are introduced have not been accounted for sufficiently in prior studies. For example, it is not unreasonable to assume that what is done under the heading of "open education" with privileged pupils may be quite different from its application in lower-class or integrated classrooms (see Chapter 9 for some results bearing on this issue). Furthermore, the classical experimental design in which all variables except the one under study are held constant may itself distort possible conclusions. In real life, what appears to be main effects may turn out to be interaction effects—often discernable only in multidimensional designs that approximate an "experimental ecology" (Bronfenbrenner, 1977) of the problem under investigation.

The organization of the present study, with all its limitations, afforded a unique opportunity to examine the effects of different kinds of intervention both singly and in combination. In the previous chapter, integration was shown to have no independent effect on achievement, a finding since replicated in two other major studies of Israeli education (Chen *et al.*, 1978; Minkovich *et al.*, 1977). Moreover, and often at odds with practitioner enthusiasm, there was some reason to suspect that the "activity" classroom was not necessarily the academic solution it was assumed to be. In what follows, this assumption is examined for different kinds of settings, including one of special interest: the middle-class school which, after integration, is organized along lines enabling a significant degree of individualized instruction, as well as enhanced opportunities for learning from peers.

Results

CROSS-SECTIONAL ANALYSIS

Lower-Class Children in Activity Classrooms

Figures 5.1 and 5.2 present the mean achievement scores in arithmetic and reading comprehension of LC and MC children in the different types of activity classrooms. Clearly, there is a differential

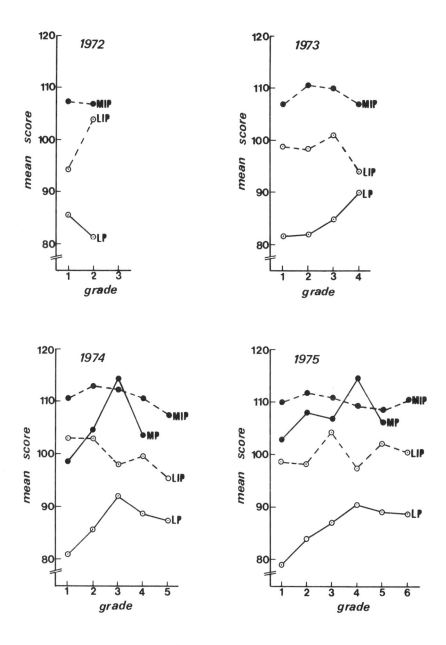

Figure 5.1. Mean arithmetic achievement of integrated and nonintegrated pupils in activity classrooms.

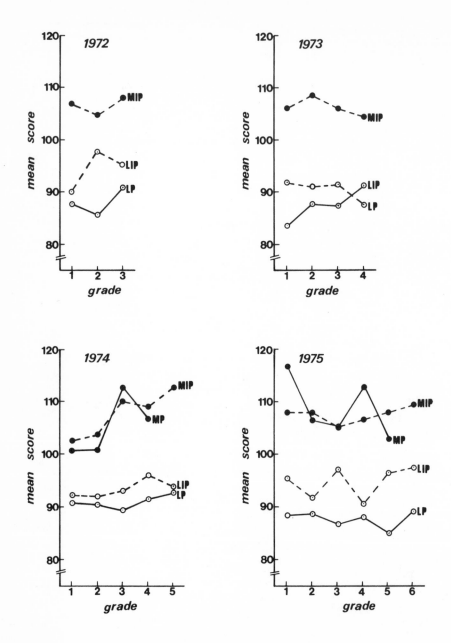

Figure 5.2. Mean reading comprehension achievement of integrated and nonintegrated pupils in activity classrooms.

effect of this educational intervention that varies with classroom social composition. Figure 5.1 indicates that:

1. LIP pupils consistently outperformed their LP peers at all grade levels in arithmetic. The mean difference between these two groups was about 13 points, or almost one standard deviation.
2. Across all grades, LIP pupils scored on average in arithmetic at or about a level equal to the standardized mean of the entire study population.
3. The difference between LP and LIP pupils remained substantial throughout the years studied. However, these differences appear to diminish somewhat with years in school. This question will be examined separately in the trend analysis.

Looking back at Figure 4.1 (arithmetic achievement in integrated and nonintegrated classrooms) and comparing it with the data in Figure 5.1 lends additional significance to the differences among the various LC pupil subgroups. Throughout their years in school, the LIP pupils were almost always the group attaining the highest achievement scores, whereas the LP pupils were just as consistently the lowest-scoring group. If the mean achievement of the LI and L subgroups can be considered characteristic of how LC children perform when no special educational intevention is applied, then the combination of integration and the "activity" classroom clearly enhanced the academic performance of LC children. What was sobering and in need of special discussion, however, was the relative deterioration in performance of LC children exposed to the activity classroom alone.

The data for reading comprehension achievement (Table 5.2) present a somewhat different picture from that for arithmetic scores. The LIP pupils still surpassed the LP pupils in reading ability on 17 out of 18 comparisons in all the years investigated. These differences all reached statistical significance (Table 5.1) but tended to be much smaller than those for arithmetic achievement (on the average of one-third standard deviation). No clear tendency for these differences to diminish over years in school could be ascertained from an examination of the mean scores. Furthermore, a comparison of Figures 4.2 and 5.2 indicates that all the LC children performed within the same general range of reading achievement.

TABLE 5.1
Analysis of Variance of Academic Achievement of Integrated and Nonintegrated Pupils in Activity Classrooms

	1972			1973			1974			1975		
	MS	df	F	MS	df	F	MS	df	F	MS	df	F
ARITHMETIC												
LC												
Grade level	134.72	1	.63	198.52	3	1.31	326.78	4	2.17	708.86	5	4.59***
Integration	17998.08	1	84.63***	20286.73	1	134.16***	21476.15	1	142.50***	31276.33	1	202.63***
Interaction	3558.57	1	16.73***	852.16	3	5.64***	1191.01	4	7.90***	504.80	5	3.27***
Residual	212.67	299		151.21	426		150.71	573		154.35	652	
MC												
Grade level							704.53	3	4.66**	142.98	4	1.15
Integration							4879.65	1	32.26***	543.21	1	4.36*
Interaction							897.33	3	5.93***	475.72	4	3.82**
Residual							151.29	555		124.62	750	
READING COMPREHENSION												
LC												
Grade level	764.64	2	3.08*	52.33	3	.32	210.77	4	1.19	171.74	5	1.04
Integration	3947.04	1	15.92***	1184.10	1	7.20**	996.91	1	5.63*	8846.71	1	53.37***
Interaction	1154.66	2	4.62**	547.04	3	3.24*	71.06	4	.40	393.39	5	2.37*
Residual	248.00	450		164.56	391		177.23	583		165.76	671	
MC												
Grade level							2472.35	3	13.84***	220.60	4	1.41
Integration							168.95	1	.95	77.44	1	.49
Interaction							131.78	3	.74	641.83	4	4.09**
Residual							178.63	583		156.96	764	

*$p < .05$
**$p < .01$
***$p < .001$

TABLE 5.2
Academic Achievement of Integrated and Nonintegrated Cohort Samples in Activity Classrooms (Mean Scores)

ARITHMETIC

Cohorts

	1970			1971					1972				1973		
	Grade 4	Grade 5	Grade 6	Grade 1	Grade 2	Grade 3	Grade 4	Grade 5	Grade 1	Grade 2	Grade 3	Grade 4	Grade 1	Grade 2	Grade 3
MC Integrated	106.8	107.9	110.6	109.6	107.7	110.7	111.7	108.7	107.1	110.7	113.4	109.2	107.1	114.2	111.8
LC Integrated	94.8	95.5	100.4	101.5	104.0	101.4	99.7	102.2	97.0	98.7	98.3	97.2	101.0	105.9	104.6
LC Nonintegrated	89.4	88.2	85.8	86.9	80.0	85.3	89.2	89.4	85.2	82.1	92.4	90.7	83.0	85.2	89.8

READING COMPREHENSION

Cohorts

	1970			1971						1972			1973		
	Grade 3	Grade 4	Grade 5	Grade 6	Grade 1	Grade 2	Grade 3	Grade 4	Grade 5	Grade 1	Grade 2	Grade 3	Grade 1	Grade 2	Grade 3
MC Integrated	109.0	105.0	112.4	110.9	104.7	107.4	110.2	108.2	106.5	108.7	110.7	106.9	105.9	104.6	106.5
LC Integrated	95.8	88.5	93.9	97.7	97.5	91.8	97.0	96.6	89.7	91.4	92.7	90.9	94.5	95.3	97.8
LC Nonintegrated	92.9	90.8	93.5	91.7	86.6	88.0	91.8	85.2	89.8	87.2	88.8	89.0	84.8	89.5	89.4

This suggests that reading comprehension scores were relatively uninfluenced by the different types of school experiences investigated in this study. Even the consistent differences between LIP and LP pupils do not offer any strong argument for a differential impact of the "activity" classroom on reading achievement.

Middle-Class Children in Activity Classrooms

The lack of an MP school in the early years of the study places some limitations on what can be said about the combined effects of integration and the activity classroom on the performance of MC children. However, in the final 2 years of the study when an MP sample was added, the MIP pupils comprised the highest-scoring subgroup. In three out of four grade levels in the 1974 sample, and in four out of five grade levels in 1975, arithmetic achievement of MIP pupils surpassed that of their peers in MP classrooms. Table 5.1 indicates that the absolute magnitude of these differences is not very great, although reaching statistical significance. (The significant interaction effect is apparently related to specific grade levels, suggesting no clear developmental pattern in the relative positions of the two types of school experience.) Patterns of results similar to those in arithmetic were also found in the reading comprehension data (Figure 5.2), although the differences were considerably smaller and statistically nonsignificant.

Comparing the data in Figures 4.1 and 5.2 indicates that MIP children performed rather consistently as well as or better than their MC peers in other settings. The crucial role of the combination of integration and the activity classroom is again highlighted, however, when considering the school performance of MI children. As already pointed out in Chapter 4, when no special educational measures were taken, MI pupils often demonstrated a decrement in academic achievement. Since all MC subgroups were initially equated on several relevant variables, there is some reason to believe that the introduction of the activity method into integrated classrooms may have played an important role in preventing similar problems in the MIP subgroup.

LONGITUDINAL ANALYSIS

In four different yearly cohorts, LIP children on the average outperformed LP pupils (Table 5.3). These differences were statisti-

TABLE 5.3

Trend Analysis of Academic Achievement of Integrated and Nonintegrated Cohort Samples in Activity Classrooms (Linear Effects Only)[a]

	Cohorts							
	1970		1971		1972		1973	
	Hyp.MS	$F_{(1.55)}$	Hyp.MS	$F_{(1.67)}$	Hyp.MS	$F_{(1.68)}$	Hyp.MS	$F_{(1.67)}$
ARITHMETIC								
LIP versus LP								
Grade	67.36	1.09	215.63	3.26	1677.56	16.89***	1039.93	11.34**
Group	1936.97	20.07***	4537.28	71.89***	2639.42	26.88***	5492.71	50.70***
Interaction	582.53	9.44**	2253.72	34.10***	1094.26	11.01**	116.64	1.28

	Cohorts							
	1970		1971		1972		1973	
	Hyp.MS	$F_{(1.57)}$	Hyp.MS	$F_{(1.75)}$	Hyp.MS	$F_{(1.53)}$	Hyp.MS	$F_{(1.69)}$
READING COMPREHENSION								
LIP versus LP								
Grade	685.72	13.32***	17.29	.22	55.80	.75	189.30	3.02
Group	48.12	.40	432.80	5.66*	.97	.01	1068.74	7.84**
Interaction	584.71	11.35**	183.80	2.35	107.28	1.44	62.72	1.00

[a] ANOVA, trend analysis, SPSS, version 7.0, 1978.

*$p < .05$
**$p < .01$
***$p < .001$

cally significant at the .001 level for arithmetic, and, in two of the four cohorts, at the .05 level for reading comprehension. The trend analysis indicates that the differences between the groups remained constant in most cases and there was no indication of a definite pattern of change as might have been inferred from the cross-sectional data presented above. Throughout the length of the study LIP and LP pupils maintained their positions as the highest and lowest LC groups irrespective of starting year. Middle-class children in MP schools were tested for only 2 years, and therefore were not included in the present analysis.

Discussion

The findings presented in this chapter lend further support to the contention raised in our introduction that it is not very useful to ask questions of the form, "Does integration—or does open education—work?" Instead, there is the need to find answers to a more deliberate and careful phrasing of the problem: Under what conditions does integrated education lead to certain effects, and what is the role of the activity classroom in this process?

Thus, for example, the findings are in partial agreement with those investigators who hold that open education programs can have a deleterious effect on the academic performance of disadvantaged children. The data, however, limit this conclusion to one very specific context—the homogeneous LC classroom—and under a further set of conditions, to be discussed later, that circumscribe such conclusions even more. A rather different rule seems to apply when the activity method is introduced into integrated classrooms. The academic benefit derived by LC children in LIP classrooms is quite obvious from Figures 5.1 and 5.2. They were the only LC group whose arithmetic performance reached the general mean of the study population. In fact, a comparison of Figures 4.1 and 5.1 indicates that LIP pupils were not very much different in their arithmetic achievement from that of at least one MC subgroup—the MI pupils. Furthermore, while the academic gap between MC and LC children remained substantially the same irrespective of classroom setting, the LIP subgroup did show a significant advance. It is interesting to note that this tendency, rather than developing gradually with years of schooling, could already be noted in first grade and was successfully maintained in later years.[1]

The results also shed some light on the feelings of ambiguity and inconsistency conveyed by studies reviewing the impact of integration and open education (St. John, 1975; Stallings, 1975). Perhaps more is being asked of such studies than can be expected. There is no reason to assume that interventions of a general nature, such as integration or open education, will influence academic performance equally across all types of subject matter. The fact that some studies report beneficial effects on mathematics tests and no effects on verbal measures does not necessarily suggest inconsistency or ambiguity in the results (St. John, 1975). Academic achievement in this study, as well as in others, was an end product of the interaction among the activity method, integration, and specific teaching approaches. The lack of uniformity in reported results is less surprising when noting that the latter two variables are generally not accounted for in any specific detail.

Moreover, there is evidence suggesting that the impact of schooling is greater in subject matter areas such as arithmetic, which are not directly tied to experiences in the home, than on others such as language and reading, which are very highly related to socialization and home background variables (Coleman, 1975).

[1]The finding that LIP pupils significantly do better on the achievement tests but show no systematic increase over time deserves some discussion. The first question is whether this group is similar to other groups, or in some way different due to a particular selection process. No selection trend is evident from the available data. Unfortunately, no IQ scores for participating children were available prior to their entering school. However, as described earlier, no meaningful differences were found among them on a number of relevant background variables at the outset of the first grade. The method for standardizing the scores seems to offer a much more plausible explanation for this phenomenon.

Standardizing raw scores for each grade level cannot explain the high performance of LIP first graders, nor the relatively low scores of other LC groups. The standardization is conducive, however, to two other trends: (a) it tends to equalize the differences between subgroups since these gaps are presented in standard deviation units, and (b) the method depresses developmental trends by determining a fixed mean score for the entire sample over grades. Whenever the gaps between them are kept fairly constant and no group develops any deviant trend of its own, no developmental change will be reflected in the mean standardized scores. In other words, the method used will approximate developmental curves only in the case of assymetric or nonparallel development of various groups.

There is, therefore, no a priori reason to expect equal results in all areas following an intervention. The lower level of reading comprehension relative to arithmetic achievement in the LIP subgroup suggests that even the "best" schools in the project did not find or employ the most comprehensive means of working with the LC child. The findings of the present study are matched, in this respect, with those of Bereiter and Englemann (1966). Even though these investigators specifically focused on the verbal behavior of LC children as a vehicle for compensatory education, the results of their program indicated a considerably greater gain in arithmetic than in language.

The discussion so far has not resolved inconsistencies in research findings, only illuminated some of the reasons behind them. The data in the present chapter, however, do tend to bring about agreement on several conclusions: (a) no academic impact of integration programs should be expected unless additional educational resources are allocated, planned for, and properly implemented; (b) seating arrangements of pupils cannot substitute for appropriate teaching methods; and (c) freedom of choice, individualization, and small group instruction are not in themselves solutions for the disadvantaged, but rather offer a set of options that may or may not be exploited for better teaching.

The last point, in particular, is important for an understanding of the effects of the activity classroom in different school settings. In the words of an experienced practitioner:

> Labels attached to an innovation can be misleading and imply a similarity and standardization. Open education often implies a lack of structure or boundaries, or an uncontrolled freedom where the teacher represses his common sense and anxiety so that the creative development of the children can change. The teacher is assured learning will somehow happen. Unfortunately, this is not the case [Andrea, 1973, p. 463].

There is a complex potential in the open education model, or what is here termed the *activity classroom,* allowing for different, sometimes conflicting, emphases in implementation. The combined effect of integration and the "activity" classroom when carried out in "good" schools represents one such complex of factors. Contrary to what was reported in the United States (Coleman *et al.,* 1966), it has been found that Israeli schools with a predominantly LC population of Asian–African origin are less well equipped than other schools in terms of both human and material resources (Minkovich *et al.*, 1977). The LIP children were thus learning in schools in which there were better teachers and a richer educational environment to begin with. Before integration, teachers in these schools had traditionally aimed at high levels of achievement, secure in the expectation that children can learn if properly taught. The advent of integration tended to make this expectation even more salient, since both teachers and MC parents were well aware of the threat of lowered academic status and reputation that might result.

On the basis of observations and interviews with school personnel, it seems to the authors that teachers in LIP classrooms interpreted and implemented the activity method in a very particular way. Their perception of the freedom and flexibility this approach offered merged with the possibility for creating more effective approaches to learning, even when measured by traditional norms and expectations. In effect, they felt they were being given a method in which they could reduce discipline and increase freedom of choice without risking what they believed to be a required level of achievement (see Chapter 9). Encouraged by their supervisors, these teachers formed a strong and cohesive group within which they constructed new instructional materials and worked on problems of translating the traditional curriculum into the terms and methods of the activity classroom. The feeling that they were part of an important development in Israeli education was supported by numerous visits of educators and others interested in the project, and by requests for advice and consultation that began coming in from all over the country.

No developments like those just described were observed among teachers of the LP children, at least some of whom tended to regard the activity method as more of a burden than a blessing. Here, a different configuration of factors was operative, as well as what seemed to be an alternative interpretation of the activity classroom's potential. These special classrooms required a great quantity of learning materials, a lower pupil–teacher ratio, and increased attention to instructional technique and teacher training. All of these were afforded to both integrated and nonintegrated project schools that adopted the activity method. However, a closer look at what actually happened revealed that the more affluent (i.e., MC) schools managed to get more of almost everything. Resources were scarce to begin with, and much depended on "improvisational" skills of principals and teachers in making up for what was otherwise unavailable. The advantage of the MC–integrated school over the LC–nonintegrated school became even more striking in this respect. In the former, active leadership that felt itself responsible for maintaining standards and implementing the special program developed. Teachers and parents in these schools were inspired to believe in the activity method, accepting it as a professional challenge and as a breakthrough in education.

In marked contrast, the LP school principals appeared to be content if they still managed to retain the level of achievement they had reached before the project began. These principals consistently conveyed the feeling that educating disadvantaged children was somehow a losing battle, while their attitude toward the activity classroom was that of extreme skepticism born of seeing many educational innovations come and go.

In this, the LP school principals were probably reflecting a general attitude of the teaching staffs in their schools. In the nationwide sample investigated by Minkovich et al. (1977), teachers in predominantly LC schools in Israel were quite pessimistic about both the academic abilities and the academic futures of their pupils. A self-fulfilling prophecy in which such attitudes led to lowered demands, lowered academic standards, and eventually a low level of pupil performance was almost inevitable (Gerard & Miller, 1975; Rist, 1970). It is highly possible that with such attitudes in the background, the introduction of the activity classroom may have served to amplify, rather than reverse the performance deficits of LC children. It was almost as if the teachers in LP classrooms saw the chance for freedom and flexibility as a substitute for learning, rather than as a renewed opportunity. The activity classroom could then be carried out under the banner of, "If they can't learn, at least they can be happy," emphasizing the elements of play, enjoyment, and "keeping busy" in a strange kind of isolation from demands for academic learning. Perhaps functioning under this banner was one of the few ways the LP classroom teachers could maintain a sense of professional integrity in the face of a program that threatened some deeply held attitudes and for which they received little support or help.

It was thus the integrated, rather than the homogeneous, schools that encouraged and legitimized demands and techniques for academic achievement within the framework of the activity method, and in fact succeeded in raising LC test scores. The findings of the present study do not obviate the possibility that under a different set of circumstances the activity classroom or similar technique might be academically effective in homogeneous LC schools. They only suggest how much events and attitudes in the experimental project were aligned against any such possibility, and how inappropriate it is to speak of the effectiveness of any intervention without taking into account the real-world context of its operation.

6

Academic Self-Concept

Re-reviewing the literature on self-image, Wylie (1974) found that most of the criticism she had levelled at the field in her classic summary (Wylie, 1961) was still valid:

> Unfortunately the kinds of methodological shortcomings one finds are the same as those I pointed out more than ten years ago:
> 1. The method used is often so vaguely indicated as to prevent interpretation and analysis and to make replication impossible....
> 2. There is very common use of measures having undemonstrated, inadequate, or even entirely unexplored construct validity....
> 3. There has been heavy reliance on R-R designs to test antecedent–consequent hypotheses.
> 4. In some studies there are not enough different control groups to hold constant or to account for all the important irrelevant variables....
> 5. In many studies there is a strong possibility of artifactual contamination between independent and dependent variables....
> 6. Various types of overgeneralization occur.... specially noteworthy ... is the heavy reliance on self-report measures as indices of the essentially nonverbal behaviors....
> 7. In some studies it appears that psychological generalizations are based on findings of unclear statistical significance....

8. Most studies have been one-shot affairs with no replication or even cross-validation of instruments....

9. The use of demographic or sociological independent variables which have unknown relevance to psychological variables precludes clear psychological interpretation of obtained association [pp. 31–32].

St. John (1975), in her review of school integration studies, added another dimension to this criticism—inconsistency of research findings. Out of 25 studies that tried to relate changes in black students' self-image to school integration, 4 show positive change, 9 indicate negative change, 7 report no relationship, and 5 provide no conclusive results. More recent reviews do not indicate an improvement in this respect (Epps, 1978; Stephan, 1978).

Awareness of all these problems, however, has not diminished the fascination of educators and researchers with the self-concept variable. Improvment of self-image has even been proposed as the major goal of integrated education. With the status of the self-concept variable in the psychological literature so problematic, assertions of this kind deserve closer examination. Why the continued recourse to a concept which has no immediate and obvious connection to learning outcomes?

Several possible explanations come to mind. A popular reason offered for the widespread academic failure among disadvantaged pupils involves the self-image as a key part of a multiphasic process in which lowered self-image leads to a defect in motivation and results in poor achievement (Gergen & Marececk, 1976). A vicious cycle ensues in which lowered achievement further decreases self-esteem. This line of reasoning suggests that improvement in self-image may be a crucial element in solving the educational problems of the disadvantaged. It is a highly attractive model, particularly since it conforms with much that is acceptable and taken for granted in current psychological thinking. If personality variables have any important role to play in the learning process, it must be in terms of forces eliciting either positive or negative motivation. Models of this kind, in addition, have a particular kind of organizational appeal. The emphasis is clearly on a problem that lies within the pupil, and which implicates the school itself only secondarily. Moreover, it is a useful conceptualization for teachers who prefer to define themselves as "educators" dealing with the "whole child," rather than as information-bearers alone.

Another reason may be that evaluating self-image is one of the methodologically simplest ways of studying personality. Self-image questionnaires are easy to administer, and the data that are obtained are in relatively simple form. Straightforward questions are asked of subjects, and the answers given to questions such as, "I am (not) (hardly) (somewhat) (very) satisfied with my performance in school," seem to have both face validity and immediate educational relevance. Information in this form is very easy to communicate to teachers and parents, and closely approximates a type of psychological reality with which they are very familiar.

In a different vein, however, the importance of the self-concept variable is somehow linked to a humane belief that every person has the right to positive self-regard. No one should either be made or allowed to feel inferior, no matter what his position relative to others may be. One version of this position is reflected in the growing contemporary concern with a right to happiness, the latter taken to be a human need of equal importance to all others. Another version can be found in the commonly held relationship between positive self-concept and good mental health. Low self-esteem is often found among persons seeking therapeutic help, and any further decline is taken to be a sign of increasing maladjustment. This correlation between self-image and mental health, based on the lower end of a range of scores, has been extended in both educational and some psychological thought to the entire distribution. Thus, any change over time in test scores can be seen as a meaningful psychological event, reflecting either maladjustment or adaptation. Monitoring self-concept, therefore, can become a major educational task. The maintenance of positive self-regard, moreover, can be transformed into an independent educational objective, equal to, or under some circumstances even superior to, other objectives such as achievement.

This emphasis on the need for positive self-regard takes on special significance in the context of integrated education. In stark contrast to the liberal notion embodied in the U.S. Supreme Court decision, for example, opponents of integration have often based their arguments on the possibility of negative personal consequences to participating minority children. Some have maintained that minority children in integrated settings may have to pay a psychological price in the coin of frustration, self-hatred, and passivity (Frankenstein, 1976; Lewin, 1935; Rist, 1970; St. John,

1971). This point of view has led in two directions. One involves a total rejection of integration as an educational tool, essentially assuming that frustrated children cannot learn. The objection to the integrated setting can stem from its potential harm to racial or ethnic pride, or from a presumed lack of congruence between the personal and intellectual styles of the majority and minority groups, the latter an argument that has been given major prominence in Israel.

Still another approach to the issue of self-concept in integrated settings assumes that something like a "trade-off" phenomenon might be involved. The image is that of a zero-sum game: For the minority pupil, improvement in one area may have to be balanced by a loss in another. Thus, even if integration led to improved achievement, educators and policy-makers would be faced with some extremely difficult decisions about the extent of the "trade off," and the amount of decline in self-image acceptable. Interestingly, it is the argument of the opponents to integration that relies heavily on a presumed positive relationship between self-concept and achievement. The "trade-off" approach, however, must assume some measure of either neutral or negative relationship in order to account for related findings. Then again, it is only in the most speculative or ideological literature on integration that one finds a third proposition: Both achievement and self-concept of minority children can be enhanced in the integrated setting. Empirically, it remains to be shown conclusively if there is a set of conditions under which this proposition can hold true.

Of all the issues raised, the one most amenable to experimental manipulation and investigation is the relationship between achievement and self-concept. Most of the other issues are much more speculative in nature, reflecting certain value judgments only few of which are directly researchable. Still, it is important to recall that all the various ideas and interpretations that have been advanced on the subject of self-concept are empirically a matter of questions on a test blank and scores that deviate from one another by a few points. Though positive or negative self-concept presents no special problem on a theoretical level, the interpretation of a specific test score, or change in scores, is quite another problem.

In the research literature, the meaning of an absolute score has generally been handled by the use of correlation coefficients that suggest how self-concept is related to other variables (e.g., St. John,

1971). The problem of changes in scores is usually a matter of assuming that practically any change over time which is related to an experimental manipulation is a meaningful one. The direction of the change, and only secondarily its magnitude, is the important factor (Rogers & Dymond, 1954). Neither of these conventions really answer some very basic questions. They continue to predominate, however, at least in part because of the lack of external and independent criteria by which a particular score, or change in scores, can be assessed. It is, after all, very difficult to measure independently and validly just how much a child is happy, feels loved by parents or teachers, or thinks highly of himself or herself.

The above discussion should not be taken to minimize the potential importance of self-image as a psychological construct. The problem is one of balance and proportion; for example, a growing body of research seems to indicate that it may be more useful to regard self-image as the outcome of complex interactions in the educational setting, rather than a specific cause (Scheirer & Krant, 1979). This conclusion was arrived at by investigators studying preschool children (Bridgeman & Shipman, 1975), junior high and high school children (Calsyn & Kenny, 1977), and young adults (Bachman & O'Mally, 1977). What these investigators have shown is that the substantial correlations often found between self-image and achievement can be better explained in terms of the correlation of these two factors with family background, prior achievement, or intelligence. These new findings cannot be explained away by assuming a simple reciprocal relationship between self-image and achievement where each equally affects the other. The picture that emerges is more unbalanced; educational outcomes have a greater role in determining self-image than the other way around. While this does not detract from the importance of the self-image variable, it points to a growing need for a different focus of investigation and interpretation than has usually been the case in the literature. For example, two issues seem to have been neglected in the otherwise rich body of existing literature on self-image. One is the issue of how self-image develops over time and in different circumstances. The other is the problem of relating self-image to independent and external criteria. Though much of the above constitutes a major problem in the study of general self-image, it is somewhat less acute for one particular facet of the self-concept, that of academic self-image. As mentioned earlier (see Chapter 3), the present chapter will relate only to this aspect of the self. It seems fair to assume that a pupil's expectations about whether or not he can usually cope with certain academic material will have some direct bearing on his actual performance in school. In principle, there are at least two school-related outcomes that can serve as independent criteria: teachers' grades and performance on objective achievement tests.

Questions to be dealt with in this chapter include

1. What are the differences in academic self-image between MC and LC children at the outset of their elementary school experience?
2. Is there a clear developmental trend to the academic self-image variable in the elementary school years?
3. Are these trends similar or different for LC and MC children?
4. Is this development affected by situational factors, such as school integration and teaching methods?

Questions related to the problem of external and independent criteria include

1. What is the relationship of academic self-concept (ASC) to teacher scores and performance on objective tests?
2. Is there any trend to these relationships over years in school?
3. Are these trends similar for LC and MC children, and are they differentially effected by tuitional factors, such as school integration and teaching methods?

Results

CROSS-SECTIONAL ANALYSIS

Academic self-concept scores for LC and MC pupils over grades in school for 4 different study years appear in Figure 6.1. Three interesting findings immediately present themselves:

1. A majority of pupils of both groups believe that they will achieve the highest possible grade in both arithmetic and reading comprehension at the end of their first year in school. In this respect they reveal no indication of lowered self-concept at the outset of their academic career.

2. There is a consistent decline in ASC scores with years in school. This decline, however, is limited in magnitude: No group of either MC or LC pupils feels itself incapable of coping with the academic assignments of the school.
3. The decline in ASC scores is consistently greater for LC as compared to MC pupils. (see Table 6.1).

On the whole, the mean scores of the LC pupils are significantly lower than those of the MC children. However, the data do not support the claim that ASC of LC children is low in either absolute or relative terms as they begin school. Practically all children in our samples began their school careers with a high estimate of their academic abilities.

Both Figure 6.1 and Table 6.1 indicate that the decline in ASC

TABLE 6.1
Academic Self-Concept of LC and MC Pupils by Year and Grade Level (Analysis of Variance)

	Arithmetic			Reading		
	MS	df	F	MS	df	F
1972						
SES	5.00	1	11.69***	4.98	1	9.45**
Grade	4.39	2	10.26***	5.81	2	11.02***
Interaction	1.42	2	3.32*	2.35	2	4.45*
1973						
SES	11.35	1	19.61***	24.82	1	51.16***
Grade	38.96	3	67.31***	35.79	3	73.79***
Interaction	1.90	3	3.28*	5.58	3	11.50***
1974						
SES	20.97	1	31.95***	19.72	1	37.57***
Grade	28.81	4	43.89***	15.61	4	29.74***
Interaction	1.73	4	2.64*	2.81	4	5.36***
1975						
SES	35.39	1	53.13***	45.14	1	88.61***
Grade	35.32	5	53.03***	24.08	5	47.27***
Interaction	.55	5	.82	1.02	5	2.00

*$p < .05$
**$p < .01$
***$p < .001$

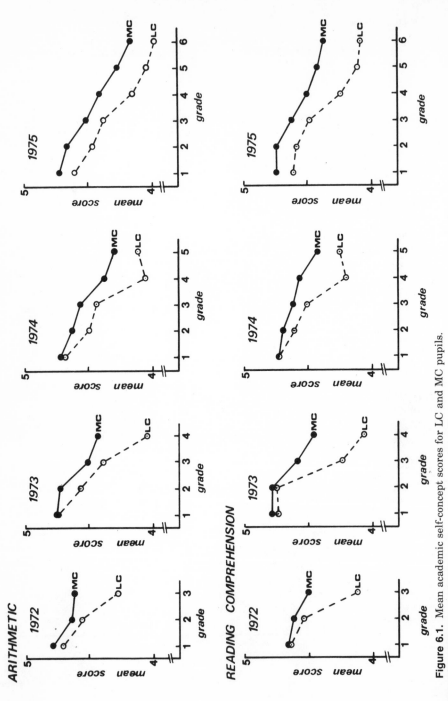

Figure 6.1. Mean academic self-concept scores for LC and MC pupils.

98

scores is significant and quite consistent for both the LC and MC children and for both academic criteria over years in school. These replications suggest that the phenomena under investigation are relatively stable. A certain amount of decrease in ASC scores seems to be a general feature of elementary school experience. The validity of the commonly held notion that decline in self-image is necessarily an indicator of some kind of maladjustment will be discussed in light of these findings.

The data presented so far discussed LC and MC children in general, across all types of schools. When examined separately for integrated versus nonintegrated schools, and for activity versus traditional classrooms, the data show no consistent differences for any subgroup. Integrated LC children tend to begin school with ASC scores slightly lower than those of comparable LC nonintegrated pupils. By the fourth grade, however, this situation is reversed. Although this interaction is significant (Eshel & Klein, 1977), the scores continue to fluctuate beyond the fourth grade. On the whole, integration does not seem to have any predictable effect on this aspect of self-image and there is no evidence for a deleterious impact on ASC of either MC or LC pupils as suggested by Coleman *et al.* (1966), St. John (1971), or Rosenberg and Simmon (1972). ASC scores were also compared with teacher grades and achievement test results both by computing correlations between measures and a comparison of means. A comparison of mean teachers' ratings presented in Table 6.2 with mean ASC scores depicted in Figure 6.1 indicates that the latter tends to parallel the former over all years in school.

ASC scores of MC pupils were quite similar to their teachers' judgments at all grade levels. LC pupils, on the other hand, consistently overestimated their academic abilities—in terms of a scale of 100, approximately 10 points above the teachers' average evaluations. However, the gap between ASC scores for the two pupil groups was considerably smaller than the differences in achievement ascribed to them by their teachers. As far as the LC children were concerned, they evidently perceived less of a difference between themselves and their MC classmates than did their teachers (a similar comparison with objective test scores could not be made because of the difference of scales employed).

In order to further assess the relationship between ASC and two criterion measures for each individual child, correlations were com-

TABLE 6.2
Teacher Scores of LC and MC Pupils by Grade Level and School Year (Means and Standard Deviation)[a]

	School years											
	1972			1973				1974				
	Grade 1	Grade 2	Grade 3	Grade 1	Grade 2	Grade 3	Grade 4	Grade 1	Grade 2	Grade 3	Grade 4	Grade 5
ARITHMETIC												
LC	4.17	4.16	3.93	4.07	3.98	4.01	3.37	4.03	3.96	3.84	3.58	3.55
	(.50)[a]	(.44)	(.71)	(.54)	(.50)	(.48)	(.75)	(.57)	(.62)	(.67)	(.69)	(.78)
MC	4.18	4.21	4.13	4.34	4.29	4.24	4.05	4.31	4.28	4.22	4.19	4.08
	(.47)	(.40)	(.53)	(.34)	(.36)	(.45)	(.66)	(.38)	(.45)	(.46)	(.56)	(.73)
READING COMPREHENSION												
LC	4.29	4.22	4.03	4.14	4.06	3.96	3.76	4.07	4.13	4.01	3.88	3.77
	(.40)	(.37)	(.75)	(.47)	(.51)	(.49)	(.64)	(.56)	(.51)	(.52)	(.55)	(.73)
MC	4.27	4.28	4.25	4.38	4.37	4.35	4.30	4.34	4.34	4.34	4.31	4.43
	(.39)	(.35)	(.43)	(.30)	(.30)	(.32)	(.54)	(.37)	(.39)	(.35)	(.43)	(.53)

[a]Numbers in parentheses are standard deviations.

puted. Table 6.3 shows that beyond sizable fluctuations in these correlations, a general trend of improvement in pupils' assessments of their actual grades emerges in most of the cases included in the table. This improvement is characteristic of both LC and MC pupils. Further dividing the study population into integrated and nonintegrated classrooms did not change this pattern.

LONGITUDINAL ANALYSIS

Mean ASC scores for MC and LC pupils in each year by cohort are presented in Figure 6.2. It is clear from this figure that the smaller sample and the intrasubject analysis do not drastically change the general patterns obtained in the cross-sectional analysis.

1. At the end of their first year in school, most children in both MC and LC groups describe themselves as fully competent to cope successfully with the academic challenge of the school.
2. There is a marked tendency for pupils of the two SES groups to lower their levels of expectations with years of schooling (see Table 6.4).
3. On a 5-point scale, however, lowered expectations do not fall below a level associated with an expectation of "good" performance.
4. LC pupils consistently evidence a lower ASC as compared to MC children. This difference tends to increase over years in school, although not for all the cohorts studied.
5. The data do not provide enough information indicating whether continued decrease in ASC is to be expected in higher grades, or whether an asymptote will be reached toward the end of elementary school.
6. Additional analysis indicated no consistent effect of integration for either LC or MC pupils.

Discussion

A decline in children's general self-image, or any one of its component aspects, is often taken as indicative of a noxious process tied to experiences of failure and frustration. In turn, this process should lead to a deterioration in the motivation to learn and achieve

TABLE 6.3
Correlations between Academic Self-Concept Scores and Academic Achievement

	Teacher scores									
	Arithmetic					Reading comprehension				
	Grade 1	Grade 2	Grade 3	Grade 4	Grade 5	Grade 1	Grade 2	Grade 3	Grade 4	Grade 5
1972										
MC	−.092	.251	.207			−.007	−.020	.304		
LC	−.047	.089	.260			.247	.287	.369		
1973										
MC	.009	.260	.409	.629		.043	.077	.220	.407	
LC	.093	.210	.293	.385		.261	.052	.240	.093	
1974										
MC	.354	.216	.317	.610	.498	.217	.173	.057	.202	.255
LC	.182	.236	.434	.552	.546	.246	.064	.195	.317	.576

102

Achievement tests

Arithmetic

	Grade 1	Grade 2	Grade 3	Grade 4	Grade 5	Grade 6
1972						
MC	.092	.202				
LC	.055	.138				
1973						
MC	.092	.241	.419	.431		
LC	.188	.162	.124	.378		
1974						
MC	.246	.209	.286	.448	.418	
LC	.099	.308	.262	.338	.341	
1975						
MC	.056	.119	.310	.369	.350	.397
LC	.233	.350	.124	.291	.057	.061

Reading comprehension

	Grade 1	Grade 2	Grade 3	Grade 4	Grade 5	Grade 6
1972						
MC	.157	.129	.190			
LC	−.072	.211	.307			
1973						
MC	.039	.229	.242	.404		
LC	.103	.097	−.001	.183		
1974						
MC	.084	.158	.233	.347	.377	
LC	.275	.138	.276	.177	.309	
1975						
MC	.069	.085	.154	.191	.297	.235
LC	.263	.346	.043	.263	.196	.307

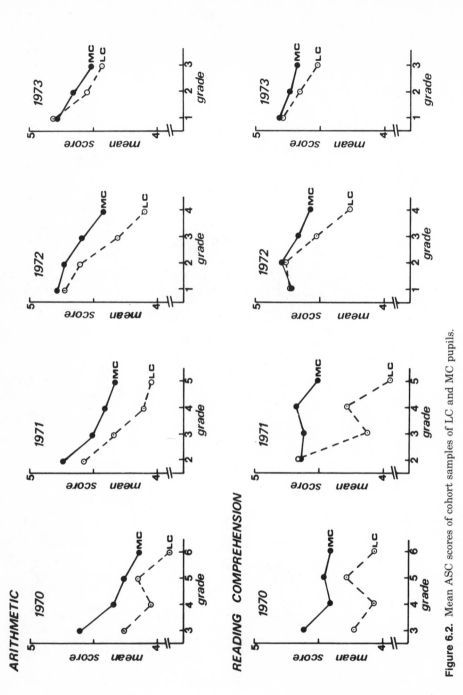

Figure 6.2. Mean ASC scores of cohort samples of LC and MC pupils.

TABLE 6.4
Trend Analysis of Academic Self-Concept of LC and MC Cohort Samples (Linear Effects Only)[a]

	Hyp.MS	F(1.394)	Hyp.MS	F(1.473)	Hyp.MS	F(1.472)	Hyp.MS	F(1.528)
ARITHMETIC								
Grade	6.36	13.06***	18.62	40.45***	26.62	54.71***	26.67	62.67***
Group	2.80	6.55*	7.35	17.49***	3.48	11.71***	.30	1.17
Interaction	.04	.09	2.16	4.69*	.42	.90	.99	2.32

	Hyp.MS	F(1.397)	Hyp.MS	F(1.472)	Hyp.MS	F(1.444)	Hyp.MS	F(1.477)
READING COMPREHENSION								
Grade	.50	1.27	2.33	5.67*	21.35	62.10***	8.08	23.86***
Group	6.23	20.64***	15.72	55.38***	2.27	13.44***	.18	3.40
Interaction	.00	.01	.13	.32	3.00	8.72**	1.31	3.88*

[a] ANOVA, trend analysis, SPSS, version 7.0, 1978.
*$p < .05$
**$p < .01$
***$p < .001$

(Dunn and Payne, 1969; Gergen and Marececk, 1976; Irwin, 1967; Katz, 1968). The findings of the present study indicate that a certain decrease in one aspect of self-image, the ASC, may be the rule, rather than the exception, throughout the early years of school. A similar trend has been suggested by several other studies (Cicirelli, 1977; Kifer, 1975; Morse, 1964; Stenner, 1975; Yamamoto, Thomas, & Karnes, 1969). Moreover, data from the present study indicate that the decrease noted is not necessarily symptomatic of a problem situation. Instead, one could as easily define it as a developmental trend toward a more realistic self-image, indicating the child's growing ability to evaluate more precisely his potential. (Additional data collected in this study, to be presented elsewhere, indicate that the same trend is to be found for general self-image as well [Persitz, 1977].)

A further aim of the study was an attempt to relate the self-image to actual behavior from which it both takes and lends psychological meaning. One aspect of this relationship can be conceived of tentatively as that of "accuracy," that is, the extent to which self-image can reflect actual behavior and/or correspond to external norms and conditions (Tagiuri, Brunner, & Blake, 1958). Two different measures of this relationship were used: (1) a comparison of group means of teachers' grades and ASC scores, and (2) correlations between these scores and achievement test results. The former would give an indication of the success of a particular pupil subgroup in approximating the mean score assigned to that subgroup by an external source of evaluation, while the latter would show how accurately any particular pupil perceives his or her relative standing in a given group as compared to relative standing on an external criterion.

The findings clearly suggest that fairly early in their school careers pupils of both groups were moving toward accurately assessing their academic abilities. LC pupils tended to overestimate their school performance in a consistent manner, as compared to their MC peers who did not differ on the average from their teachers' ratings. This finding closely resembles earlier studies in the United States (Gibbey & Gabler, 1967). However, the individual child in both groups steadily improved in ability to perceive accurately his or her performance as reflected by external criteria.

The finding that decrease in ASC and increase in accuracy of judgment go hand in hand, rather than being mutually exclusive, further points to the conclusion that this decrease may reflect more realistic self-perceptions. The latter findings also emphasize the importance of reexamining the assumption that school failure among LC children is often predetermined by low levels of self-esteem brought from the home into the school setting (Ausubel & Ausubel, 1963; Deutsch, 1960).

First-grade LC pupils in the study began their school career with an elevated academic self-image, and maintained it in this fashion for several years so that their self-perceptions were consistently overestimates of objective ability measures. Whether or not and how such patterns are eventually resolved remains an open and problematic area in the self-concept literature. At the very least, it should be noted that all children in the study began school with quite an optimistic academic outlook, and managed to remain that way for quite a while. While the decrease in ASC score for the LC children was greater than that for MC pupils, the total range of decline for both groups was only between grades of A and B. A negative self-image (i.e., underestimation of actual grade) was not reflected in the group comparison data.

There does not seem to be any simple or direct way to relate differences in self-image scores to children's academic performance. No evidence was found in the present study that academic self-evaluation had any bearing on academic performance, provided that ASC did not fall below a minimal level that could still be regarded positively. Thus, for instance, mean differences in test scores between subgroups (see Chapters 4 and 5) were not reflected in the ASC data.

Decreased ASC of LC pupils following integration was assumed by several authorities to be a "price" demanded from these children in return for the benefits of learning in a middle-class desegregated school (Coleman *et al.,* 1966; St. John, 1971). The present study tends to agree with later studies suggesting that integration in itself cannot systematically be related to changes in self-image without taking into account additional variables (see, for instance, Epps, 1975; St. John, 1975; Scheirer & Krant, 1979; Stephan, 1978). Self-concept has been described in many works as an intervening variable responsible for heightened or lowered motivation to learn. Examination of the relevant literature suggests that this assumption had rarely been put to direct test, and had been taken for granted on a theoretical basis. Both the data presented in this chapter and recent studies in the United States (Bridgeman & Shipman, 1978; Calsyn & Kenny, 1977; Rubin, Dorle, & Sandidge, 1977) suggest that this reasoning is not well founded. More often than not, self-concept seems to reflect the child's level of achievement rather than to cause it. It may be more profitable, therefore, to regard general and academic self-concept as one possible educational outcome that may be important in its own right, and relieve it of exaggerated responsibility for other, more task-oriented outcomes.

7

Social Interaction in
the Integrated Classroom

Anyone surveying the vast number of integration programs and evaluation studies must eventually be struck by a curious lack of connection between theory, policy, and practice. Policy-makers appear to act, at least in part, on the assumption that close relations between majority and minority groups are an ultimate goal, and that certain classroom arrangements will help to bring this goal about. Creating opportunities for heightened social interaction is taken to be an important step toward improving attitudes, self-evaluations, and ethnic relationships.

Social scientists, on the other hand, have long pointed out that attitude change and improved relationships are not always guaranteed outcomes. In fact, a complex set of preconditions must be fulfilled for such outcomes to take place. Many of these preconditions are well-known (Allport, 1954; Amir, 1976; Schofield, 1978) even though all their possible permutations have not been fully studied. Even though not always clearly stated, the implication is that if such preconditions are not met, there is very little chance for change and improvement.

It is all the more striking, therefore, to note that policy-makers and educational personnel are not the only ones who seem to expect positive changes as a direct result of placing different children together in the classroom. Social scientists who evaluate school integration programs also appear to hold these beliefs. How else can one explain the fact that sociometric and attitude change studies are routinely made part of evaluations, even though there is little or no specification of relevant conditions such as those mentioned above?

A summary of the research on interracial attitudes and relations in the desegregated school between 1937-73 (St. John, 1975) fails to find any clear trend following integration. Several studies did find improvement in racial attitudes, whereas others report deterioration attributable to racial contact. A third group of studies indicates no clear effect of racial mix on attitude tests, observed behavior, or sociometric choices. Further division of those projects studied into mandatory or voluntary desegregation programs carried out in local neighborhoods versus busing, or those designed as cross-sectional versus longitudinal studies, does not seem to alter the conclusion that "in sum, comparative studies of the racial attitudes of segregated and desegregated school children are inconclusive [St. John, 1975, p. 80]."

More recent reviews do not suggest any improvement in the overall picture. To cite one reviewer: "The only finding which emerges consistently from sociometric and observational studies in desegregated schools is that students interact more with others of their own group than would be expected if race were not an important grouping criterion [Schofield, 1978, p. 334]." Rather than leading to increased cohesiveness within integrated groups, desegregation seems often to contribute to a deepening cleavage between them, at least at the sociometric level. This is true whether traditional or more sophisticated methods of measurement are used (Singleton & Asher, 1977). The largest desegregation study of its kind (Gerard & Miller, 1975) found that the gap in sociometric status between the majority and the minority in the desegregated classroom tends to increase substantially with time.

It is difficult to determine to what extent these trends represent the integrated setting per se, and how much they reflect racial relationships typical of the United States. Data collected in Israel are still too piecemeal and inconsistent to answer these questions conclusively. One recent Israeli study found sociometric preferences to be fairly evenly distributed among junior high pupils of European and Asian–African origin. Preference for one's own group, although consistent, remained at a rather moderate level (Levin & Chen, 1977). Another study conducted with ninth graders suggested quite a different trend. Pupils of Asian–African origin were more accepting of their own ethnic group after spending a year in desegregated classrooms. No similar change was found for Western peers. The authors maintain that these trends do not stem from an in-group isolationism characterized by rejection of the high-status group. Pupils of Asian–African origin evidenced no change in their evaluation of their Western peers (Amir, Sharan, Bizman, Rivner, & Ben-Ari, 1977). This positive picture is not replicated in another study by the same research group in which MC pupils tended to refrain from informal interaction with LC peers (Amir, Rich, & Ben-Ari, 1978). Thus, there is no strong evidence in Israel supporting the egalitarian assumption that integrating school children will necessarily have a beneficial effect on their social relationships and their ethnic attitudes, without any other specific interventions.

The most prevalent theory on racial relations is Allport's (1954) contact theory. Three major conditions are suggested as prerequisites for improved ethnic relations in a biracial group: (1) status equality of the two groups, (2) interaction leading to mutual interdependence, and (3) favorable attitudes toward interracial association. Experimental studies suggest that when these conditions are not met, black students tend to exhibit low performance on intellectual tasks and to behave submissively toward both white peers and experimenters (Katz, 1967). On the other hand, it is assumed that "acceptance of Negroes by white peers and adults should have a social facilitation effect upon their ability to learn, by motivating them to adhere to white standards of academic performance [p. 149]."

A growing number of studies suggest that meeting these conditions can be a sound basis for improved ethnic relations, at least in a very controlled environment. This was demonstrated by equalizing status (Schofield, 1978; Schofield & Sagar, 1977), by creating interdependence (Aronson, Blaney, Sikes, Stephan, & Snapp, 1975; Blaney, Stephan, Rosenfield, Aronson, & Sikes, 1977), by inverting status order through granting the power of expertise to minority members (Cohen, Lockheed, & Lohman, 1976; Sharan, Cohen, & Elchanani, 1977) and by interteam competition (DeVries, Edwards, & Slavin, 1978; Slavin, 1979).

There is no question about the theoretical importance of these findings to the study of integration. Yet, hardly any suggestion is presented in this body of research concerning the implementation of these ideas within the school system. A set of translation rules seems essential to test the implied assumption that these experiments closely simulate the learning process.

In quite another vein, however, the problem of social interaction in the school setting is discussed in terms of actual classroom conditions and the possibility of creating opportunities for intensive and meaningful cooperative relationships among children. Open education settings, for example, are designed to provide conditions for fostering such relationships by making them an essential part of the learning process. Whether or not these conditions are actually implemented, however, depends on the specific nature of the program, on the one hand, and the way it is understood and implemented by the teacher, on the other. Hallinan (1976), for example, finds that "open classrooms have the advantage of decreasing the number of social isolates, of increasing the longevity of friendships, and fostering a more uniform distribution of popularity." However, contrary to expectations, "children in traditional classrooms tend to have more friends on the average [p. 263]." This pattern is not generally applicable to all open classrooms. There is at least one study suggesting that decreasing the limitations on free social interaction in the class will not necessarily result in improved intergroup relations. An investigation of sociometric preferences in integrated and open schools (Bartel, Bartel, & Grill, 1973) did not indicate any positive effect of the British Infant School type of education on mutual acceptance of black and white elementary school children. Racial cleavage was found on each of the four sociometric criteria used. Furthermore, this cleavage tended to increase steadily after the first year or two in school. In terms of positive friendship choices, an almost total racial polarization was found by the fourth grade.

The assumed relationship between open education and development of more meaningful interactions among pupils rests upon the structural properties of the former: "The single most important factor affecting the formation and development of friendship among children is the amount of interaction in which they engage [Hallinan, 1976, p. 286]." If indeed this is the case, there is no question about the expected social results of the activity classroom. Hallinan neglected, however, to mention the quality of these interactions. There is ample reason to believe that the nature of intergroup contacts and their interaction with the wider social setting are far more important than their quantity alone (Amir, 1976; Klein & Eshel, 1977).

In the present chapter we examine the effects of school integration and of the "activity" method on cross-group and own-group sociometric preferences. Rather than comparing the choice patterns before and after integration, we sought to determine what changes over time characterize each of the subgroups studied (as far as cross-sectional data will allow). In addition, we were interested in examining different areas of classroom activity, and their relation to sociometric patterns in different classroom settings.

Method

The sociometric questionnaire administered in the present study included two questions. The first question represented the academic interaction among pupils, whereas the second probed for the social aspect. The organization of learning in the classroom was decided in all our classrooms by the school. The appropriate sociometric question, therefore, was hypothetical, that is, "List three children with whom you would like to study." The social interaction in the pupils' free time enabled a more factual question: "Who are the three children with whom you play most often at recess time?" All pupils from the third grade up in all of the study schools who were present on testing days were administered the questionnaire in the last month of every school year.

The sample in the present chapter is comprised of 55 integrated classrooms, for which sociometric data are available. Twenty-eight of these classrooms were designated as "activity" classes, and the rest, 27, were taught by traditional methods. Two sociometric scores were computed for each class for each consecutive year. The first represents choice of MC pupils by LC peers, the second being the opposite preference. These scores were corrected for the proportion of LC to MC pupils in the classroom, and for the total number of pupils enrolled in it. In what follows, only data from school year 1975 are analyzed and presented.

Results

For obvious reasons, only integrated classrooms were included in the present analysis, since they are the only ones relevant to the issue of cross-group sociometric choice. Three measures were employed: the total number of choices received by an individual pupil; the number of choices assigned by the pupil's LC peers; and the number of choices allocated by the pupil's MC peers. The three scores were computed by subtracting expected choices from those actually received, where the former was based on the relative number of the participants in each classroom.

The results of two-way analyses of variance on each of the three measures were computed separately for LC and MC pupils who participated in the study in the 1975 school year (see Table 7.1). As indicated by these analyses there is no significant effect of grade level on patterns of sociometric choice for any of the measures of groups investigated. In other words, sociometric choices allocated to both MC and LC pupils are fairly constant over time. Intergroup friendship patterns in our study did not seem to be appreciably affected by the amount of time spent together in integrated classrooms. Furthermore, the pupils studied tended, for the most part, to prefer members of their own group as friends. This rule, however, did not seem to apply in one case: An examination of the means indicated that LC pupils tended to prefer their MC peers as companions in learning over members of their own group (Figure 7.1). Their choices for play companions, however, were very much an in-group matter. Further comparisons showed that the distributions of choices made by the two groups were somewhat different. LC pupils tended to spread their friendship choices more equally between MC and LC peers as compared to choices made by MC pupils in the same classrooms. The mean difference between one- and other-group choices made by LC children was .18 for the play measure, and .22 for the learning measure. For MC children these figures were respectively .76 and 1.23, or a difference in group choice at least four times larger than that for LC children. Thus, while LC children appeared willing to select friends among all their peers, the MC pupils clearly preferred members of their own group. MC pupils, however, did differentiate between play and learning friendships, much the same as the LC children did: They were more willing to

TABLE 7.1
Sociometric Choices by Grade Level and SES (Analysis of Variance)

	Total choices received			Choices allocated by LC			Choices allocated by MC		
	MS	df	F	MS	df	F	MS	df	F
Play companion									
Grade level	.77	3	.20	.77	3	.87	1.00	3	.40
SES	104.66	1	26.51***	9.24	1	10.32***	168.80	1	67.01***
Interaction	1.94	3	.49	1.08	3	1.21	1.13	3	.45
Residual	3.95	1467	—	.90	1467	—	2.52	1467	—
Study companion									
Grade level	2370.13	3	7.79***	.89	3	.76	.47	3	.12
SES	1206.15	1	3.96*	13.89	1	11.74***	342.82	1	110.18***
Interaction	584.74	3	1.80	1.39	3	1.20	3.42	3	.87
Residual	1381.12	1467	—	1.17	1467	—	3.93	1467	—

*$p < .05$
***$p < .001$

115

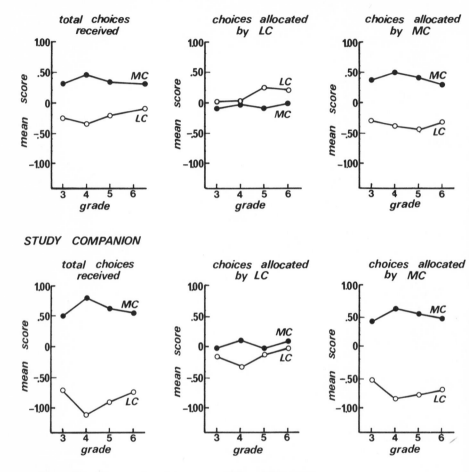

Figure 7.1. Mean sociometric scores of LC and MC pupils.

consider their LC classmates for play situations than for learning together.

Additional differentiation of the classrooms in the sample into activity-oriented and conventional categories revealed mean differences that were quite consistent, although not statistically significant in all the comparisons involved (see Table 7.2). Both MIP and LIP pupils tended to receive more choices from others in their classrooms as compared to MI and LI children. In other words,

TABLE 7.2
Sociometric Scores of Pupils in Integrated Classrooms by SES, Grade Level, and Method of Teaching (Means and Standard Deviations)[a]

	Lower class								Middle class							
	Grade 3		Grade 4		Grade 5		Grade 6		Grade 3		Grade 4		Grade 5		Grade 6	
	LIP	LI	LIP	LI	LIP	LI	LIP	LI	MIP	MI	MIP	MI	MIP	MI	MIP	MI
Play companion																
Total choices received[a]	-.34 (1.66)	-.23 (1.82)	-.50 (1.81)	-.18 (1.76)	.24 (1.48)	-.75 (1.71)	.21 (1.62)	-.18 (1.56)	.34 (2.04)	.26 (2.13)	.55 (2.24)	.40 (2.10)	.40 (1.77)	.31 (2.35)	.41 (1.56)	.03 (2.22)
Choices allocated by LC	.02 (.86)	.02 (1.04)	.06 (.96)	.01 (1.21)	.64 (1.21)	-.24 (.57)	.37 (1.05)	-.18 (.40)	-.13 (.81)	-.09 (.95)	.27 (1.23)	-.24 (1.01)	-.14 (.78)	-.06 (.78)	-.09 (.65)	.09 (.90)
Choices allocated by MC	-.36 (1.16)	-.26 (1.28)	-.56 (1.36)	-.19 (1.32)	-.40 (1.19)	-.49 (1.47)	-.16 (1.18)	-.72 (1.57)	.44 (1.64)	.33 (1.67)	.28 (1.56)	.63 (1.73)	.54 (1.53)	.34 (1.85)	.50 (1.50)	-.07 (1.86)
Study companion																
Total choices received	-.97 (1.55)	-.56 (1.85)	-1.02 (1.51)	-.12 (1.69)	-.66 (1.60)	-1.20 (1.48)	-.71 (1.33)	-.82 (2.49)	.70 (3.08)	.39 (2.78)	.83 (2.82)	.78 (3.16)	.91 (2.92)	.43 (2.64)	.85 (2.39)	.09 (2.60)
Choices allocated by LC	-.15 (.89)	-.18 (1.06)	-.14 (1.00)	-.43 (.96)	.06 (1.08)	-.34 (.60)	.00 (.96)	-.12 (.84)	-.01 (1.05)	-.04 (1.11)	.33 (1.40)	-.02 (1.22)	.14 (1.21)	-.05 (.91)	.11 (.93)	.10 (1.04)
Choices allocated by MC	-.82 (1.10)	-.38 (1.48)	-.88 (.97)	-.79 (1.26)	-.73 (1.19)	-.86 (1.29)	-.71 (.91)	-.71 (2.12)	.52 (2.36)	.36 (2.13)	.51 (1.95)	.68 (2.37)	.69 (2.14)	.43 (2.12)	.70 (2.09)	.00 (2.27)

[a] Numbers in parentheses are standard deviations.

117

TABLE 7.3
Sociometric Choices of LC and MC Pupils by Grade Level and Classroom "Openness" (Analysis of Variance)

	Sociometric measures								
	Total choices received			Choices allocated by LC			Choices allocated by MC		
	MS	df	F	MS	df	F	MS	df	F
Play companion									
Grade level	492.68	3	2.85*	.81	3	.80	.39	3	.23
Group (LIP–LI)	34608.75	1	200.05***	8.90	1	8.85***	.27	1	.16
Interaction	2370.88	3	13.71***	4.38	3	4.35**	2.54	3	1.52
Residual	173.00	386	—	1.01	386	—	1.68	386	—
Grade level	314.20	3	1.88	.46	3	.56	2.01	3	.72
Group (MIP–MI)	146097.14	1	872.41***	1.48	1	1.80	2.16	1	.77
Interaction	7762.46	3	46.35***	6.49	3	7.90***	8.58	3	3.06*
Residual	167.46	1073	—	.82	1073	—	2.81	1073	—
Study companion									
Grade level	446.58	3	2.70*	.75	3	.81	1.60	3	1.01
Group (LIP–LI)	27595.46	1	166.98***	4.42	1	4.81*	1.67	1	1.06
Interaction	2064.02	3	12.49***	.75	3	.81	1.53	3	.97
Residual	165.27	386	—	1.37	386	—	1.58	386	—
Grade level	502.12	3	2.92*	1.15	3	.92	2.54	3	.53
Group (MIP–MI)	132267.52	1	770.11***	6.21	1	4.98*	9.88	1	2.07
Interaction	10835.02	3	63.09***	1.62	3	1.30	7.38	3	1.55
Residual	171.75	1073	—	1.25	1073	—	4.77	1073	—

pupils in open classrooms tended to have more friends than similar peers in conventional integrated classrooms.

Table 7.3 presents two way analyses of variance of these findings from which something can be learned regarding the nature of the relationships among grade level, activity versus conventional classroom, and sociometric choice. Only on the total choices measure were consistent and significant interaction effects to be found between classroom openness and grade level. Examination of the means (Table 7.2) indicates that on the whole the higher the grade level the more LIP and MIP pupils were chosen by all their peers. The reverse was the case for pupils in conventional classes.

Discussion

The data presented in this chapter suggest that—not unlike the situation discussed regarding achievement outcomes—the formal act of bringing children together in integrated classrooms was not a sufficient condition for changing patterns of social interaction. When no specific measures are taken to improve cooperation and communication, then, as reported in earlier studies (Gerard & Miller, 1975; Singleton & Asher, 1977), there is reason to expect either no change or possibly even an increase in own-group preference over time. Teachers and principals in the project schools knew that they were dealing with a problem of major social significance. Beyond this awareness, however, they were given very few conceptual or technical tools to enable them actively to do something about the issue. The disparity between goals and actual implementation was consistently evident—a theme that recurs over and over again in integration programs.

At the heart of the matter is the fact that integrated schools are assigned the task of implementing an ideal social reality which the society at large has had difficulty in living up to. The belief is implicit that schools have the proper means for taking on this responsibility and producing the desired change. And yet, detailed curricula for integrated classrooms hardly exist, either in the United States or Israel. Manuals for improving cross-group attitudes in the integrated school are a relatively new phenomenon, and clearly convey the feeling that ultimate goals are easier to talk about than the means required for achieving them (see, for example, Forehand & Ragosta, 1976; Miller, 1977).

In the absence of specific intervention methodologies, what the many studies of attitude change and sociometric status are actually examining are forms of cross-group encounter under a wide variety of possible conditions. Two such conditions were represented in the present study: integrated classrooms with traditional educational treatment, and integrated classrooms with a special educational intervention. In neither case was there any special preparation as might be called for by theoretical considerations for attitude change—for example, provision of equal status as a prerequisite for effective group life. However, the particular emphasis on social interaction built into the activity classroom model did seem to have an effect on intergroup relationships, and one which appeared to increase over years in school. The fact that such an increase consistently took place within a specific type of educational intervention shows that there are important potentialities yet to be explored.

The possible relationship between this indication of improved social atmosphere in the activity classrooms, and the achievement gains in these same classrooms will be taken up in Chapter 9. What is most interesting about the data for all classrooms is that LC pupils were accepting of the majority as well as themselves, whereas their MC classmates maintained their distance. Despite these different perceptions, the classrooms continued to function, and in some, the LC children benefited academically in a significant way.

Two conclusions might be drawn in this regard. First, equality of status may be an optimal end state which is not necessarily a condition for effective performance in an integrated group. While equality of status may be important in some settings, it may be overemphasized as far as the elementary school situation is concerned. Unfortunately, no attitudinal data were collected in parallel with sociometric choices. There is no way of judging whether or not stereotypes were reduced and nonmembers of either group were regarded more positively or realistically.

Furthermore, the findings in Chapter 5 suggest that the total acceptance of LC pupils as equals by their MC peers is not a necessary precondition for the improved academic performance of LC children in integrated elementary school classrooms. Nor does this lack of total acceptance seem to lead to any significant decrement in self-evaluation, as suggested by the self-image data in Chapter 6.

Several students of integration maintain that relative status within the classroom rather than extramural status is the important factor in school group relations. The present data further suggest that actual differences between subgroups in home background or academic achievement may not be the crucial issue in the elementary school setting. It is rather the way that differences are perceived that may make the difference. If the minority is "unconcerned" with disparities perceived by the majority, either because of an unwillingness to look at the facts, or because majority attitudes are neither salient nor provocative, there is the possibility that no feeling of inferiority will develop, and no negative emotional tone will be associated with integration.

Nothing in either the self-image data or classroom observations suggested that integrated elementary school classrooms in the study were in any way especially problematic. Classrooms functioned fairly smoothly, children felt fairly good about themselves and their academic accomplishments, and LC children even widened the net of their friendships and associations (even though this was not always reciprocated). What were effectively created were settings in which children of different backgrounds worked together with a minimum of friction, with little evidence of psychological "prices" to be paid, and, under special conditions, with some academic benefit to the minority. For some, this might be a hopeful sign—a basis upon which to build a set of further academic interventions. For others, the lack of total reciprocity in sociometric choice might only underline the false assumptions and illusions contained in integration programs.

Those who follow the latter line of reasoning might despair about how far removed the school situation is from actually changing economic, political, and social realities. Some analysts further suggest that creating equality in the school will fail to contribute significantly to solving inequality in adult life. Such problems can be solved only by establishing political control over the major economic and social institutions that shape society (Jencks, 1972). In this light, the data presented above are painfully far from an ideal of integration. But if classroom interactions can be characterized as tolerant, and under certain conditions and for some outcomes even as effective, how shall the problem be defined?

8

Classroom Composition and the Activity-Oriented Method

In Chapters 4 and 5, the major finding was of a positive impact upon the achievement of LC children in integrated classrooms employing a special activity method. This interaction raises many questions about what actually took place in such classrooms: Do they represent clear-cut educational and psychological alternatives and if so, can anything be said about the mechanism of their influence?

A brief description of the activity classroom and its rationale were presented in Chapter 5. When the project was initiated, however, there was only general agreement on the major features of such classes, and only vague definitions of themes and methods had been formulated. The Ministry of Education and Culture had little experience in fielding similar programs. Officials could offer only marginal help in defining objectives, while simultaneously being wary of letting university experts take over and run the program their own way. At the outset, it was a group of kindergarten supervisors who provided project teachers with support, reassurance, and advice. Drawing upon a progressive educational tradition of their own, these supervisors promoted a rationale for the activity classroom that was quite similar to that of the British Infant School:

> to allow (children) to be themselves and to develop in the way and the pace appropriate to them. It tries to equalize opportunities and to compensate for handicaps. It lays special stress on individual discovery, on first hand experience and on opportunities for creative work. It insists that knowledge does not fall into neatly separate compartments and that work and play are not opposite but complementary. A child brought up in such an atmosphere at all stages of his education has some hope of becoming a balanced and mature adult and of being able to live in, to contribute to, and to look critically at the society of which he forms a part [Plowden Report, 1967, pp. 187–188].

That this became a guiding ideology for the project teachers can be seen from the remarks of the teachers themselves when commenting on their programs:

> The activity method is based on the following principles:
> a. Attention to the individual pupil's needs and encouragement of his initiative and independence.
> b. Varied and creative activity of children carried out as an intrinsic response to an atmosphere of freedom.
> c. A balanced combination of total classroom involvement with individual and small group activities.
> d. Joining academic learning with play carried out both inside and outside the classroom.
> e. The guiding principle is that of learning through doing and the general development of social and academic behaviors [Naftali, 1973, p. 38].

In an important sense, the project teachers were identifying with a movement of radical school change that centered on the concept of "openness." Hill (1975), in an excellent discussion of the many forms this concept can take, has pointed out some of its more significant variations. *Procedural openness,* for example, does not challenge the conventional aims and concepts of education. Its main objective is to create "a rich environment of possible activities ... to lead the child into activities that call for the same skills that formal school seeks [Hill, 1975, p. 6]."

Normative openness, on the other hand, represents another trend which "challenges the right of the teacher to be anything more than a facilitator, responsive to the expressed desires of the learner. . . . The intention [is] to leave the individual free to develop in any direction he chooses [Hill, 1975, p. 7]." Hill rightly points out that this version of "freedom" is far from being value free. Both the cognitive developmental approach and the moralistic–religious point of view are rejected as possible major educational aims. A third emphasis in the literature on open education can be named *revolutionary openness*. Hill "views the availability to oppressed classes of genuine openness in curriculum choices and learning procedures as a means of accelerating cataclysmic social change [Hill, 1975, p. 9]."

The project classrooms were thus to be aligned with an ideology of change that could take on a wide variety of meanings and forms depending not only on the intention of planners but on situational possibilities and constraints, as well. Hill's analysis leaves the impression that whatever form of openness develops is the result of a rational decision-making process: methods are fit to objectives and the result is a clear and consistent educational approach. What actually happens in the field, however, may be quite another matter.

The activity classroom, and the guiding ideology initially available, had to be shaped around a framework containing two incontrovertable elements: the traditional school and the new fact of integration. This rapidly led to the development of incongruities and conflicts that affected the solutions and compromises finally hit upon.

For example, there is the deeply rooted traditional Jewish emphasis on academic excellence and achievement. A constant feature of the Israeli school system, this emphasis and its structured demands stand in partial contradiction to some current trends in Anglo-American versions of open education. One can find in the latter serious attempts to foster individual growth and freedom even at the expense of academic achievement (McPartland & Epstein, 1977). More than one definition of "openness" requires the teacher to purposely ignore many elements of academic performance and allow maximum leeway for pupils to do whatever they feel like doing. However much this trend may be an inappropriate exaggeration (Kozol, 1972), it is rather easy to derive from general prescriptions and repeated emphasis on "discovery," "experience," "growth," "play," and so forth. Inevitably, the teachers in the project had to reconcile such trends with concerns voiced by parents, supervisors, and peers for achievement. The project schools themselves were reputed to be among the academic best in the community. Maintaining this reputation was an everyday issue—a real, if unspoken, goal of all concerned. What, then, would be the form of reconciliation with a philosophy of "openness"?

The presence of two distinct subgroups in the same classroom, separated by large differences in academic ability, further complicated the problem. The activity method had been chosen to guarantee a maximum of individualized attention and tailored instruction. As ideals, these were evident in the general definitions of "openness" as quoted above. Translation into actual practice, however, was almost totally unknown in the country. The project teachers, starting almost from scratch, had to develop methods and materials with very little outside help. Moreover, the implementation of what they produced called for changing many conventional practices and redefining standard ways of considering such normative issues in the classroom as order, discipline, noise level, and attention. On the other hand, the fact of integration demanded that major consideration be given to cooperation and cohesiveness among all the pupils. There was a deep, if rather vague, appreciation that the success or failure of the project was linked to how well the children got along with one another and the kind of group portrait they presented.

The project teachers, then, were faced with a staggering task of setting priorities, assimilating a new teaching method, developing materials, and juggling a long list of demands. In attempting to look more closely at what actually took place in the classrooms, the authors tried to take into account the fact that there were at least two sets of both theoretical and applied questions. The first had to do with introducing an innovation into a traditional setting. This would require mapping the dimensions and features of the "standard" Israeli classroom in order to ascertain which of these, if any, changed after modifications had been made.

The second set of questions places the problem in a cross-cultural context: How far can an educational method, developed under one type of cultural and social conditions, be translated into the language and cultural atmosphere of another society? This would require an analysis of the major features of the innovation itself, a detailing of the behaviors and practices linked to these features, and an examination of what happens as the innovation either fits in or comes into conflict with prevailing standards and norms.

Cross-cultural studies seemed to suggest a rather straightforward answer to the second set of questions. There is, for example, a striking resemblance between the ways in which teachers in Great Britain and the United States understood and implemented the "open" method (Walberg & Thomas, 1972). This similarity was maintained even though the open education movement has been far from uniform (Weber, 1971) and despite significant differences between the educational systems of the two countries. But this is an obvious case. The United States and Britain share a great many values and beliefs, the overlap becoming more pronounced with the passing years. It would be difficult to imagine "openness" flourishing in societies that, for one reason or another, would play down values such as individuality, nonuniform self-fulfillment, creativity, or person (not group) responsibility. While Israeli society is similar to the United States and Great Britain in many respects, there are enough points of divergence to suggest that the introduction of an "open" philosophy would meet with some resistance. This might express itself in outright rejection of some parts of the idea, along with changing the meaning and/or practice of others. At the point of beginning classroom observations, however, it was difficult to predict exactly the shape and form the resistance might take.

As the project developed, visitors to the "activity" classes came away with a strong impression of a warm, busy, noisy, and highly charged atmosphere. Children seemed to go about their work eagerly with evident satisfaction and joy. There were many times when pupils failed to notice the sound of the bell calling for recess and play time. Teachers proudly pointed out LC pupils working and reading on their own, and MC children in the same setting carrying out complex self-assigned projects. Most striking of all was the report of children in the "activity" classrooms who actually enjoyed being in school.

With little more than this public enthusiasm to go on, educational authorities in Jerusalem began encouraging the rapid spread of the activity model—in at least its outward, organizational form—to many other elementary schools. But the more the model and the enthusiasm for it were circulated, the more important it became to describe specifically how these classrooms differed from others in the study and what it was about them that was affecting various aspects of pupil performance. Almost despite the enthusiasm being generated, the authors felt that many features of conventional teaching were being retained, that some interesting compromises were being struck between the desire to innovate and the pressure for traditional goals, and that the background characteristics of the pupils might continue to play a significant role in perceived success and satisfaction.

Method

In recent years, many different scales and observation schedules have been employed in examining open education settings. None of them, however, seemed to capture adequately many of the issues and problems of the "activity" classroom in Israel as just discussed. A new observation schedule was devised by the authors. Called the Open Classroom Scale (OCS), it consisted of 70 items describing observable behaviors of teachers and pupils, with each item to be rated on a 4-point scale. The items were drawn from both the Anglo-American and Israeli literature on open education, as well as from extensive interviews with teachers and program supervisors. Several different types of information were sought; elements of teaching methods other researchers had found to differentiate between "good" and "poor" teachers (Minuchin, Biber, Shapiro, & Zimiles, 1969; Rosenshine & Furst, 1971); behaviors generally associated with major dimensions of open educational practice; physical aspects of classroom organization and design; and behaviors characteristic of "traditional" classroom practice in Israel.

The OCS scale is presented in Table 8.1. Items included in the OCS were selected by pretest from a larger pool, omitting those items for which low agreement between observers was obtained. The media correlation between judges across items in the final version of the OCS was tetrachoric $r = .76$, after scores had been regrouped dichotomously (yes/no; present/absent). Most of the items required a minimal amount of inference, in most cases asking the observer to note what was clearly either present or absent in the classroom.

Forty-six first-, second-, and third-grade elementary school classrooms were included in the observational study. These classrooms comprised about 50% of the total number of classrooms in the 1975 study sample. Half of the 46 were employing conventional methods of teaching, while the other half were identified by principals and supervisors as activity classrooms. The 46 were composed of 26 classrooms that were integrated, 14 with only LC pupils, and 6 with only MC children.

TABLE 8.1
Open Classroom Scale (OCS)

1. Classroom has fixed sitting arrangements.
2. Classroom contains working corners utilized by pupils.
3. Pupils can seclude themselves.
4. Corridors and other school space utilized for learning.
5. Class is decorated with standard materials.
6. Teacher prepared and set classroom exhibition.
7. Pupil products used for classroom decoration.
8. Pupil productions displayed are stereotyped.
9. Available working corners: science, arithmetic, art, play, language, library, others
   _____.
10. Materials available: toys, games, plasticine, clay, wood, straw, paper, drawing materials, others _____.
11. Teacher employs materials provided by pupils.
12. Instruction carried out in small groups.
13. Various subjects learned simultaneously.
14. Individual pupils learn subject matter in different ways.
15. Different groups learn subject matter in different ways.
16. Class as a whole participates in choice of subject matter.
17. Small groups participate in choice of subject matter.
18. Individual pupil allowed choice of subject matter.
19. Recesses are on fixed schedule and obligatory.
20. Teacher primarily lectures to class.
21. Teacher employs open ended questions.
22. Teacher elicits mainly expected answers.
23. Teacher accepts divergent answers.
24. Teacher encourages questions.
25. Teacher elaborates subject matter through pupil produced examples.
26. Teacher relates subject matter to pupils' experience.
27. Teacher conveys general concepts and conclusions.
28. Utilization of concrete teaching aids.
29. Pupils are led to analysis and application of general concepts.
30. Teacher encourages artistic expression.
31. Teacher encourages creative writing.
32. Teacher encourages independent information seeking.
33. Teacher individualizes contact with pupils.
34. Teacher activates passive pupils in group assignments.
35. Teacher activates passive pupils in regular lessons.
36. Pupils express own feelings and thoughts.
37. Teacher elaborates on pupils' feelings.
38. Teacher freely dispenses positive rewards.
39. Teacher negatively rewards incorrect answers.
40. Teacher encourages cooperation among pupils.
41. Teacher clearly specifies task requirements.
42. Teacher presents subject matter in variegated ways.
43. Teacher tries to make lesson interesting.
44. Classes clearly defined with specific goals.

(cont.)

Table 8.1 (*cont.*)

---

45. Teacher summarizes at end of lesson.
46. Teacher corrects errors.
47. Teacher stresses silence during lessons.
48. Teacher unable to control class.
49. Extent to which punishment is used.
50. Pupils allowed to circulate freely.
51. Percentage of teacher time spent on disciplinary problems.
52. Percentage of teacher time devoted to instruction.
53. Percentage of teacher time spent in talking to class.
54. Tasks in small groups require cooperative efforts.
55. Pupils involved in learning tasks beyond what is required.
56. Pupils initiate information search.
57. Pupils frequently ask questions.
58. Active participation of pupils in class.
59. Number of pupils not following lesson's content.
60. Number of pupils inattentive.
61. Number of pupils not participating in formal instruction.
62. Number of pupils not participating in group work.
63. Number of pupils failing to complete assignments.
64. Pupils have free access to teacher.
65. Pupils finishing ahead of time disturb their peers.
66. Pupils offer help to slower peers.
67. Pupils engage in self-initiated activity.
68. Total class disturbance.
69. Isolated pupils' disturbances.
70. Pupils utilize different materials in class work.

Classroom observations were carried out in the second half of 1975 by a group of six observers trained by the authors. Two observers carried out independent observations in each classroom for 2 complete school days, spaced about 2 weeks apart. The observational unit was the classroom as a whole, rather than individual pupils, and the total school day rather than time samples were used as a basis for arriving at a classroom profile. Observers were randomly paired throughout the study. Mean scores of all four observations were used as classroom scores in the following analysis.

Results

The first question to be considered in the analysis was: Were the "activity" classrooms discernably different from others, and in what ways? The effect of grade level on the observed behaviors was tested by means of a one-way analysis of variance. No significant differences were found, and all three grade levels were combined in further examination of the data.

A two-way ANOVA program was used to determine the contribution of integration, of "openness," and of the interaction between them to differences in classroom operation. Most of the significant differences among individual items were found to be an effect of the interaction between the two variables (see Table 8.2). Further examination of the cell means indicated that the least number of "open" characteristics was to be found in conventional classrooms with a homogeneous MC population (M); the most "open" classes, on the other hand, were designated activity classrooms also with MC children alone (MP). Table 8.2 indicates, for example, that it was the presence of MC children in the classrooms designated as activity that helped account for teachers offering free choice of learning activity or free access to the teacher herself. Teachers in activity classrooms tended to limit privileges of this kind—much the same as conventional classroom teachers—unless they had MC pupils to work with.

TABLE 8.2
OCS Items with Significant Interactions between Activity Methods and Integration

	$F(2.45)$
9A. Science corner available.	4.995*
9C. Art corner available.	3.469*
9D. Play corner available.	4.237*
12. Instruction carried out in small groups.	3.871*
13. Various subjects learned simultaneously.	3.538*
16. Class as a whole participates in choice of subject matter.	4.810*
17. Small groups allowed choice of subject matter.	4.061*
18. Individual pupil allowed choice of subject matter.	3.828*
54. Tasks in small groups require cooperative effort.	3.495*
64. Pupils have free access to teacher.	5.598**
66. Pupils offer help to slower peers.	3.394*
67. Pupils engage in self-initiated activity.	4.913*
70. Pupils utilize different materials in classroom work.	5.112*

*$p < .05$
**$p < .01$

Pupils in all the activity classrooms were organized into small groups. In fact, this focus on small-group learning has been found to distinguish somewhat between Israeli and Anglo-American versions of the "open" classroom (Klein and Eshel, in press). Examination of the means indicates, however, that cooperation and team work, and not just small-group organization, were positively correlated with the percentage of MC children in the activity classroom. The same was true for the number of different facilities available to pupils, and for actual use of materials and special project corners.

An additional seven items were directly related to integration (Table 8.3). Evidently, homogeneous classroooms, *even when designated as "activity" classes,* were more conventionally run. Teachers in LC classrooms employed mainly frontal methods of instruction, spent most of their time in lecturing, and limited themselves and their pupils to the expected and the ordinary. Initiative, cooperation, and spontaneity were not particularly evident, and many pupils failed to follow and understand learning tasks. This appeared to be the case even when various structural changes in classroom procedure were noted (see Table 8.4).

Six items were related to the activity method above (Table 8.4). These items seem to refer primarily to organizational changes in the classroom and different forms of pupil participation.

TABLE 8.3
OCS Items Significantly Related to Integration

	$F(2,45)$
5. Classes decorated with standard materials.	4.706*
6. Teacher prepares and sets classroom exhibitions.[a]	4.771*
8. Pupil productions displayed are stereotyped.[a]	4.256*
22. Teacher elicits mainly expected answers.[a]	7.245**
40. Teacher encourages cooperation.	3.575*
53. Percentage of teacher time spent in talking to class.[a]	7.467**
63. Number of pupils failing to complete assignment.[a]	7.686***

[a] Negatively scored items.
*$p < .05$
**$p < .001$

TABLE 8.4
OCS Items Significantly Related to the Activity Method

	$F(1,45)$
19. Recesses are on fixed schedule and obligatory. [a]	9.103**
40. Teacher encourages cooperation among pupils.	11.153**
45. Teacher summarizes at end of lesson.	5.429*
47. Teacher stresses silence during lessons. [a]	10.387**
55. Pupils involved in learning beyond what is required.	5.091*
60. Number of pupils inattentive. [a]	4.336*
61. Number of pupils not participating in formal instruction (as opposed to informal).	8.851**

[a] Negatively scored items.
*$p < .05$
**$p < .01$

Discussion

Perhaps the clearest finding of all was that on the majority of OCS items differences between types of classrooms were not significant. Whatever differences between activity and conventional classrooms existed were found to be—to use Hill's (1975) typology—mostly "procedural": changes that do not challenge the conventional aims of education. Physical rearrangement of classrooms and the grouping of pupils for learning tasks were rapidly put into practice. But little change was noted in reducing teacher control, or allowing pupils to participate in curriculum development. The activity classrooms observed had many organizational features in common with other versions of "open" education. Here the similarity, for the most part, ended. There did not seem to be any sign of attempts to change substantially basic educational premises. Many of the traditional emphases of the Israeli school system were retained (i.e., press for achievement, order and discipline, total control over curriculum, teaching in the hands of teachers alone, etc.; see Table 8.5, Factor V, Conventional Teaching) with only those innovations that created minimal disturbance sanctioned.

Moreover, this limited type of implementation seemed to be itself dependent on the presence of certain kinds of pupils in the classroom—MC children who were, by definition and common agreement, highly motivated and capable. Teachers in homogeneous LC classrooms appeared to have the most difficulty in implementing and maintaining aspects of the activity method. Taken together, these findings suggest that either the training and support received by project teachers focused largely on the types of responses and behavior characteristic of MC children, or that the behavior MC children displayed was more congruent with what teachers expected to follow from implementing activity methods. Walberg and Thomas (1975) have also found that a greater degree of "openness" is achieved in predominantly middle-class classrooms. These results do not say anything about either the appropriateness or feasibility of "open" methodology with lower-class children. But, they do suggest that implementing open education in lower-class settings requires a great deal of planning and investment, and less reliance on day-to-day ingenuity and inventiveness.

The fact that LC children were exposed to some of the benefits of the activity classrooms in the project mainly when they contained a majority of MC pupils hints at some of the reasons for our findings in Chapters 4 and 5. This will be discussed later when examining the relationship of classroom to outcome variables. At this point, however, it is important to try to understand some of the factors contributing to the particular form the activity classroom took on in the project. It was both an exciting and ambivalent combination of events. Project school principals adopted the new method rather willingly. They expected to gain either from the new method or from the extra teaching hours and materials allocated to them. The activity teachers were given the task of carrying out the innovation and making the best of it with rather minimal instruction or advice. They carried out this task with a mixture of pride and anxiety. For most of them, it was a new and quite flattering experience to be part of an educational experiment and to be frequently visited by distinguished guests. And yet the very fact of constantly being in the limelight could itself be anxiety provoking.

The project was a source of new professional challenges and even identity for the activity classroom teachers; their commitment, if anything, strengthened as they gave up their free time for no extra reward. But taking on new tasks and self-perceptions also meant breaking down traditional behaviors, particularly those from which they had long derived their sense of competence and professionalism. Though the peer group of teachers offered some support in making this transition (Binyamini & Sherf, 1977), it was far from effortless and smooth. Sarason (1971) has described the processes that usually take place whenever significant changes in curriculum or classroom organization are introduced. Analyzing the case of the introduction of new math into elementary schools, he found teachers reacting in one of two ways. "On the one hand they were caught up in the enthusiasm surrounding the change and looked forward to the stimulation expected from what was intellectually novel and prestigeful; on the other hand, they became increasingly anxious as it became increasingly clear that... learning it to a criterion of security was not going to be easy, and that summer workshops... might expose their insecurity and... their inadequacy [Sarason, 1971, p. 42]."

Intensive interviews with teachers who participated in the integration project bear witness to their acute and ambivalent reactions to the new role forced upon them (Sherf, 1973). A new professional identity had to be found in order to cope with their situation. Threats and promises embedded in this identity, most likely, formed the core conflict the teachers had to face in the project and helped provide one motivation to interpret and construct the teaching assignment in various conflict-reducing ways.

That these methods of conflict-reduction are often limited and stereotyped in the school situation has been well-documented by Sarason (1971). Examining the process of educational change, Sarason suggests that it is frequently characterized by: (1) introduction of ideas coming primarily from outside of school culture; (2) little or no attention paid to the characteristics of this culture and its social and psychological correlates, and (3) an assumption that change could be achieved independent of any change in these characteristics. Very little weight is typically given to considering who the agents of change really are—nor to how much their own attitudes, beliefs, anxieties, and actual competence will determine the outcome of any program.

But this structural pressure to resolve the strains of almost any innovation is only one aspect of the problem. Another is more closely linked to specific meanings attached to the concept of "openness." A developing society such as Israel, intent on political, economic, and cultural stability, will tend to concentrate on promoting values centering on collective responsibility and committment. Wide-ranging experiments in self-actualization and individual expression may be regarded not only as extravagant, but even as potentially harmful. As Berger, Berger, and Kellner (1973) point out, both affluence and security are among the necessary conditions for trying out a variety of educational objectives—including the possibility that not everyone need be prepared to serve the country and become a useful citizen as generally defined. For many reasons, such a pluralistic approach to education could not easily take root in Israel. The continuing primacy of collective goals and pressing manpower and social needs serves to guarantee a relatively high level of uniformity in the educational system. This uniformity is sanctioned and maintained by a centralized educational authority. Only innovations which do not call some very basic issues into question have any chance of succeeding.

Classroom Variables and Achievement

After characterizing the similarities and differences among open and conventional classrooms, a further attempt was made to relate specific kinds of classroom inputs and events to achievement measures employed in the study. This was done by means of a factor analysis[1] of the OCS, based on correlations for the entire sample. The mean performance of MC and LC children on several measures in each classroom was then related to factor scores[2] obtained for that particular setting.

The OCS contained both items relating to inputs of various kinds—teacher behaviors, curriculum, physical organization, methods, and materials, etc.—and what might be called outcome variables—pupil concentration and attention, deportment, cooperation, and participation. A factor analysis was carried out only on input items (60 out of 80 items), yielding six orthogonal factors. Table 8.5 lists these six factors and the items comprising them.

---

[1]The centroid method of factor analysis was employed.

[2]All items with a factor loading of .40 and above were included in the factor. The factor score was obtained by assigning equal weight to all items thus included. The median for each item was then computed and ratings for each classroom were rescored as either above or below the median. The factor score for each classroom is thus the arithmetical sum of all items in a given factor scored above the median divided by the total number of items in the factor.

TABLE 8.5
Factors and Factor Loadings of OCS Observations

I. Openness

18.	Individual pupil allowed choice of subject matter.	.537
21.	Teacher employs open-ended questions.	.622
23.	Teacher accepts divergent answers.	.744
24.	Teacher encourages questions.	.767
25.	Teacher elaborates subject matter through pupil-produced examples.	.621
26.	Teacher relates subject matter to pupils' experiences.	.789
36.	Pupils express own feelings and thoughts.	.807
37.	Teacher elaborates on pupils' own feelings.	.663
38.	Teacher freely dispenses positive rewards.	.427
50.	Pupils allowed to freely circulate.	.486
65.	Pupils have free access to teacher.	.612

II. Freedom of expression

3.	Pupils can seclude themselves.	.598
7.	Pupil productions used for classroom decoration.	.583
13.	Various subjects learned simultaneously.	.671
31.	Teacher encourages creative writing.	.537
39.	Teacher negatively rewards incorrect answers.	-.504
47.	Teacher stresses silence during lessons.	-.626
50.	Pupils allowed to freely circulate.	.578
51.	Percentage of teacher's time spent on disciplinary problems.	-.479
65.	Pupils have free access to teacher.	.405

III. Activity grouping

11.	Teacher employs materials provided by pupils.	.414
12.	Instruction carried out in small groups.	.688
28.	Utilization of concrete teaching aids.	.630
40.	Teacher encourages cooperation among pupils.	.402
42.	Teacher presents subject matter in variegated ways.	.433
54.	Tasks in small groups require cooperative efforts.	.676
71.	Pupils utilize different material in classroom work.	.865

IV. Freedom of choice

13.	Various subjects learned simultaneously.	.434
15.	Different groups learn subject matter in different ways.	.733
16.	Class as a whole participates in choice of subject matter.	.705
19.	Small groups participate in choice of subject matter.	.766
41.	Teacher clearly specifies task requirements.	-.666

V. Reasoning

27.	Teacher conveys general concepts and conclusions.	.771
29.	Pupils are led to analysis and application of general concepts.	.841
43.	Teacher tries to make lesson interesting and successfully understood.	.415
46.	Teacher corrects errors.	-.455

VI. Conventional teaching

2.	Classroom contains learning corners utilized by pupils.	-.596
4.	Corridors and other school space utilized for learning.	-.435
8.	Pupil productions displayed are stereotyped.	.411
10.	Number of different materials available.	-.440
14.	Individual pupils learn subject matter in different ways.	-.585
19.	Recesses are fixed and obligatory.	.688
20.	Teacher primarily lectures to class.	.593
22.	Teacher elicits mainly expected answers.	.734
30.	Teacher encourages artistic expression.	-.445
33.	Teacher individualizes contacts with pupils.	-.418
42.	Teacher presents subject matter in variegated ways.	-.439
46.	Teacher corrects errors.	-.611
52.	Percentage of teacher time devoted to instruction.	-.396
53.	Percentage of teacher time spent in talking to entire class.	.496

Factor I—"Openness"— focuses on teaching practices associated with open classroom methodology. Factor II is concerned with provision of self-expression and personal freedom for pupils. Factor III characterizes the particular form of small-group learning employed in the activity classrooms. The implementation of freedom of choice specifically in the learning process and curriculum is defined by Factor IV. Factor V, on the other hand, contains items associated with conventional, as opposed to "open", classroom practice (many items are negatively scored). Factor VI conveys the authors' original intention to examine teaching practices specifically related to cognitive as opposed to rote learning.

Table 8.6 presents the results of zero-order correlations computed separately for MC and LC pupils relating OCS factors to mean achievement scores. As far as the LC children are concerned, the only factor significantly related to their achievement is Factor III, the activity form of small-group instruction. All other types of classroom events and methods—either conventional or "open"— appear unrelated to academic achievement. For MC pupils, on the other hand, almost all of the factors describing various aspects of open-classroom practice are related to language scores, although not to arithmetic.

Factor III is an amalgam of organizational, interpersonal, and instructional matters. With the small group as a framework, the teacher designs and implements curricular tasks in ways that em-

TABLE 8.6
Correlations between OCS Factors and Mean Achievement Scores (Pearson r)

OCS factors	Reading comprehension		Arithmetic	
	MC	LC	MC	LC
Openness	.519**	.182	.067	.034
Free expression	.340	.124	.133	.046
Group work	.404*	.413*	.184	.364*
Free choice	.371*	.197	−.107	−.106
Reasoning	.557**	.184	.165	.228
Frontal teaching	−.319	−.188	−.078	−.155
	$N=32$	$N=40$	$N=32$	$N=40$

*$p < .05$
**$p < .01$

phasize pupil motivation and an appropriate fit between the pupils' present level of ability and the materials presented to him or her. The items suggest greater attention to the specific needs of pupils, a movement away from standard or stereotyped instruction, and the use of the small group as a medium for reinforcing learning. The combination of practices in Factor III indicates how the small group might serve as a vehicle for more particularized kinds of instruction and involvement. The relation between Factor III and achievement for LC pupils thus parallels the common finding in the compensatory education literature (Bereiter & Englemann, 1966; Stallings, 1975) that improvement in the achievement of disadvantaged pupils is most often associated with pointed, "tailor-made" instruction that emphasizes specific gains in a given subject area.

The present finding differs, however, in that such improvement in learning in the Israeli context usually took place in classrooms stressing many of the features of "openness." American studies have tended to draw sharp distinctions between open-type programs and more focused instructional models. It is only the latter that are usually found to contribute significantly to higher achievement among the disadvantaged. The implication is that focused learning and "openness" are, if not incompatible, at least difficult to link together in any feasible way. The project teachers evidently did find ways of establishing a link—even if, as noted previously, many other aspects of open methodology were difficult to observe in their classrooms. The ideology of the "activity" method seems to have encouraged teachers to explore and develop more individualized and involving forms of instruction, thus breaking down some of the stereotyped regularities and expectations of conventional methods. The importance of high achievement as a goal in Israeli schools helped guarantee that whatever modifications were made would center on academic learning issues, and only secondarily on the more intrapersonal and self-expressive aspects of the ideology.

Important to note, however, is the fact that it was the presence of MC children in the classroom that contributed to teachers' effectively implementing the "activity" method. This amplifies the finding in Chapter 5 of the *interaction* between integration and activity method relating to improved achievement in LC pupils. It also raises an interesting question of the possible reinforcing effects of certain types of pupils and pupil responses on teacher behavior and initiative.

Summary

Classroom observations conducted in the sixth year of the project indicated that activity classrooms were not entirely dissimilar from conventional classrooms. Teachers in all settings maintained a great deal of control, stressed achievement and order, and were reluctant to allow pupils any significant role in determining curriculum and learning tasks.

The activity classrooms did differ, however, in several procedural ways. These included physical organization to allow for more freedom of movement and access to the teacher, greater variability in materials and methods, and division of the class into small learning groups. Implementing these changes, however, seemed to be contingent on the presence of MC children in the classroom. The LP classrooms included in the study were hardly different from conventional disadvantaged settings. Indeed, as suggested previously (Chapter 5) the introduction of some features of "openness" into homogeneous disadvantaged settings may have interfered even with conventional academic goals and practices.

The major contribution of the activity approach to improved academic achievement centered on the combination of small-group learning and variability of available methods and meterials. Put simply, the activity method seemed to afford more possibilities for reaching the individual disadvantaged child and his specific learning problems. The special method helped keep academic issues prominent, while providing teachers with a rationale for exploring changes and modifications. This suggests that there may have been nothing particularly magical about the activity method itself. Focus on specific learning problems, variation in methods and materials, cooperative learning, stress on activity, greater individualized contact—all these elements might be organized and implemented in several different ways, some, perhaps, very different from the model adopted in the project (see, for example, Sharan, in press).

The centrality of what are mainly pedagogical innovations to the improved learning of the LC children in the study only highlights again the fragility of such programs. Neither intergroup contact nor improved physical and "atmospheric" classroom conditions—the relatively obvious things to accomplish in integration programs—alone lead to academic change. Those elements that do impact are directly tied to teacher preparation, knowledge, and skill, as well as a system of technical and motivational supports to help guarantee them. Yet, the history of the project contains too many instances of the educational authorities looking upon the additional supervision, curriculum development, and allocation of teacher time necessary as extravagant and superfluous. The bureaucratic pull to a least common denominator of implementation remains a paradoxical accompaniment of all such innovations.

9

Discussion

The results of our study showed how integration was associated with significant improvement in the achievement of disadvantaged children *under some conditions, but not under others.* The finding was obtained consistently over 5 years of evaluation and with different pupil cohorts, thus lending a fair amount of credibility to the effects described. However, we have emphasized repeatedly that the findings cannot be understood as an abstract playing out of psychological laws, but must be seen in their complex linkage to a particular configuration of events that went to make up the project under investigation. In preceding chapters, we have tried to bring these events into focus—sometimes descriptively, sometimes speculatively—and consider them along with the data and the statistical analyses. In this we closely follow Cronbach (1975) in his eloquent analysis of the search for lawfulness in the social sciences. Cronbach's insistence on the importance of "local conditions" in the interpretation of complex interactions forces one to consider the temporal and tentative nature of findings such as ours. As he puts it:

> Generalizations decay. At one time a conclusion describes the existing
> situation well, at a later time, it accounts for very little variance, and
> ultimately, it is valid only as history. The half-life of an empirical proposi-
> tion may be great or small. The more open a system, the shorter the
> half-life of relations within it are likely to be [Cronbach, 1975, p. 123].

What we would like to do in these final pages is to set our
findings into a context which includes both the changing social
world in which the experimental program took place and some ideas
about the psychological processes involved in the classroom. We will
argue that there are few general or universal laws applicable to all
instances of social integration programs. Each instance presents, at
least in part, a unique set of events that must be understood in its
own right. Moreover, we will propose that such sets of events are
dynamic, that is, developing and often fragile constructions whose
form, content, and meaning are always open to change. The results,
as Cronbach further suggests, are less conclusions than they are
working hypotheses: ways of asking questions about program implementation, and provision of insights and feedback about particular local conditions. While this approach may put severe limits on
the generalizability of our findings, it may help clarify some of the
more problematic aspects of the debate around school integration.

As pointed out in Chapter 1, the underlying theme of integration in Israel is the concept of *Mizug Galuyot,* (the "intermingling of
the exiles"). We have written elsewhere (Klein & Eshel, 1977) that
the translation of this concept in the Israeli school system can best
be understood by the general notion of *assimilation:* the induction of
a minority into the ways of thinking and behaving of a majority
such that the minority becomes increasingly indistinguishable. This
can be seen as the educational component of the much broader
societal goal of *absorption* of large numbers of immigrants into the
ongoing political, economic, and social life of the country. These are
the ideals adhered to by all segments of the population and the
symbols not only of national aspiration and unity, but of national
survival.

However, all of these concepts—*Mizug Galuyot,* assimilation,
absorption—were rarely defined operationally or thought through
in consistent detail. They conveyed a general hope that differences
among cultural and social groups would vanish. Much confidence
was placed in a melting-pot notion that the power of the desire for
national unity, the sharing of a common fate, participation in

everyday life, and even the passage of time would lead inevitably to "real" integration. While many things were done both to and for new immigrant groups, they were part of an almost paternalistic approach that tended to gloss over critical problems of relating deeds to slogans.

This combination of high aspirations and failure to appreciate developing anamolies was also evident in the schools. In the early years of the state, the schools performed an extremely impressive job not only of providing education for all, but also of making considerable inroads into the serious educational gaps between Western and Asian–African immigrant groups. These achievements, however, in the paradoxical manner well-described by sociologists (Eisenstadt, 1977; Inbar & Adler, 1977) often served to highlight, rather than do away with differences. The rise of bureaucracy, patterns of urban segregation, privatization, increased technological sophistication—all these helped make whatever gains had been achieved often appear minimal, and not infrequently, even dysfunctional. Major social institutions, including the school system, on the other hand, became increasingly complacent, still officially pronouncing their attachment to symbols of national identity, but more and more concerned with everyday problems of survival and consolidation of power.

It is in this context that one can begin to understand the peculiar significance of the cry for school integration raised by the parents in the poorer neighborhood, as well as the initial incredulity of school and public officials. The latter thought that they were already doing what was required of them, whereas the parents were convinced that what was being done was neither fast, total, nor effective enough. The demand for school integration was thus a way of reiterating the official goals of absorption, assimilation, and "intermingling," but now fleshing out the bare framework of these goals with more specific concerns for improved educational and social *impact*. This was not a call for revolution, but a demand for intensification of what the schools were thought to be for in the first place—agencies of assimilation and absorption leading to more effective social participation. Whatever the elements making for such participation, it was the high-status, middle-class schools that were perceived as having more of them. Issues of equal social status, "togetherness," and possible attitude change often associated with democratic versions of school integration were hardly mentioned. In an often unspoken way, the national ideology was assumed to cover these issues. No one would question that these goals were always, in some ultimate sense, related to whatever would be done in the schools, or what would eventually be available in the society.[1] The focus, therefore, was on what could actually and immediately be gained in the classroom: better grades, better behavior, better appearance, the feeling and pride of being part of a high-status enterprise. The rest would somehow take care of itself, or be implicit in whatever readjustments might be gained on a day-to-day basis.

The emergence of school integration in Israel thus crystallized around at least two major tendencies. One was the common cause of all parties concerned to play down the more painful aspects of ethnic disparities. No undue public emphasis should be given to such differences for fear of encouraging feelings of inferiority, or projecting a situation of animosity and estrangement. The second tendency was the shared belief that the means for effecting change were already available: They just had not been implemented widely or thoroughly enough. Neither of these tendencies was particularly conducive to rethinking or restructuring the educational process itself. Instead, the impression was that some right combination of unspecified socioeducational chemistry and ample time would provide the conditions for beneficial effects to take place. When the Israeli government adopted school integration (at the junior high school level) as a national policy through the School Reform Program of 1969, it promised two positive results almost as a matter of course: improved academic achievement and positive social relations. While much was done in terms of redistricting and building a network of new comprehensive high schools, little pedagogical preparation or programming went into the undertaking.

The picture of high-sounding rhetoric and relative inaction as far as the educational process was concerned has also been typical of

[1]It is interesting to note that as the debate on integration in Israeli schools has widened, it is the middle-class, Western origin parents who have increasingly focused on the supposed failure of integrated schools to change attitudes and promote "togetherness" as a reason for questioning the whole enterprise. Two versions of this argument are prominent: One views this failure as a sort of "fact of life" which only time can change (and thus conservatively opposes any major integration programs); the other sees this failure as symptomatic of a majority "plot" to coopt the minority while offering little in return—and thus an argument for a much more radical restructuring of the society.

the American experience with integration. But many of the ideologized elements and priorities are different from the Israeli situation, and require separate examination.

It is interesting, for example, to contrast the rather "minimalist" approach to change in the Israeli version—one that does not stress such things as major personality or attitude change, status shifts, or radical institutional restructuring—with several of the perspectives prominent in the American literature on school integration. Schofield (1978) has recently critically appraised these models, and in what follows, we rely on her excellent review. This will help to highlight some conceptual distinctions to be developed further later in the chapter.

In trying to explain why integration should have a positive impact on the disadvantaged child, theorists in America have generally focused on major changes in self and other perception brought about by alterations, often radical ones, in the conditions of interpersonal and intergroup contact. Allport's contact theory (and the important variations offered by Pettigrew [1973] and Cook [1963]) stresses both the need for structuring conditions leading to equal status and mutual interdependence, and the disconfirmation of prevailing stereotyped beliefs. Katz (1967) highlights the importance of changing self-attributes of motivation and competence, while Cohen (1975) goes even further in emphasizing the need for at least a temporary reversal of superior and subordinate roles to effect positive relations. In order to prove their respective points, these authors have developed quite sophisticated experimental demonstrations of their hypotheses. Under controlled laboratory conditions, some striking changes in attitude and behavior have been demonstrated.

There are several characteristics that these theoretical approaches have in common. For one, they are all *reconstructive,* that is, change is not expected unless serious alterations are made in the situation of intergroup contact. Taking these changes out of the laboratory and projecting them onto institutions or society as a whole illustrates just how far-reaching such changes would be. In fact, the changes proposed, such as status reversals, mutual interdependence, and equal access to sources of social status, are almost a vision of what an ideally integrated society might be—here collapsed onto the simpler microcosm of the experimental situation. In effect, these theories go a long way toward identifying an end state with the means for achieving it. Unfortunately, they offer little guidance as to how to go about reproducing laboratory conditions on a larger bureaucratic and social scale.[2]

Second, while stressing situational effects, all the theorists, either implicitly or explicitly, emphasize the *intrapersonal* dimension of change. Attitudes, self-esteem, motivation, orientation, and so on are key factors in any formula for improvement. The sheer number of attitude and personality measures in desegregation research underlines the importance attributed to profound and lasting changes in the person as both prerequisite and outcome of effective programs. This suggests that whatever problems are to be overcome are deeply rooted in the individual. They cannot easily be exorcised by some simple form of situational rearrangement. The impression is of historical residues in the individual of pain, hurt, distortion, and prejudice that have become part of the fabric of being, and, as such, must act as a conservative brake on various forms of intervention.

It is surprising, therefore, how little the enormity of undertaking major personality change has found expression in the structure of various desegregation programs in the United States. Researchers look for change in individuals within programs where little is done beyond bringing the two groups together. Finding no results or equivocal ones, they may complain that not enough has been done and the "real" depths have not been reached; or that the problem is too complex for this type of intervention; or that personality issues are irrelevant and potentially biasing. Something of this perplexity is aptly caught by Miller and Gerard (1976) when, after finding no results of a desegregation program, they wrote:

> In retrospect, the whole model we were using—the idea that academic achievement would change as personality changed—embodied on arrogant, white middle-class ideology that was and probably still is useless as a means of improving minority education. Personality, after all, would be a terribly difficult thing to change even if we were sure it was a key factor in performance [p. 100].

---

[2]The lack of much thought given to the problem of translating lab results to the "real" world can lead to serious distortion. Rosenwald (1975) has neatly documented the vicissitudes of the T-group and sensitivity training movement. Its proponents long insisted that they were reproducing and affecting the real world with their special techniques. Many years of equivocal research results led to a withdrawal from such claims and substitution of more personalized goals. The net effect, as Rosenwald points out, is to leave the "real" world more or less the way it is.

The emphasis on social reconstruction and major intrapersonal change we note in American theorists reflects a social and historical context for integration in which prejudice runs deep and is ordered by often rigid social arrangements. In their paradigms, these theorists project a set of *distal* goals—a reordering of relationships, feelings, and behaviors that typify how the world might be different. These goals are not steps in a process, nor do they suggest a developmental sequence. They are versions of what should be, and thus focus heavily on outcomes. Almost paradoxically, they convey both despair about the deeply ingrained nature of the problem, and an optimism about the rational and technical ability to solve it.

Perhaps these are some of the reasons why so little attention has been paid in American studies to more *proximal* concerns: the everyday life of classrooms, the non-Utopian and imperfect attempts to make something happen which may fall far short of ultimate aims, but may nonetheless be part of an important process. Only rarely, as for example in the work of Aronson *et al.* (1975), Cohen *et al.* (1976), or Slavin (1979) is there a consideration of making changes in actual classroom behavior within the limits of what is attainable in such settings. The steady preoccupation of theorists, tacticians, and political allies of integration with *distal* goals—in the absence of any clear set of transformational rules as to how to get from the present "imperfect" to the future "perfect"—seems to lead to cycles of optimism and disappointment followed either by retreat or renewed calls for faith and action.

In Israel, there is no lack of *distal* concerns and goals—of social justice, of equality, of cultural creation, and many others. What may be different from the American experience with integration is that, at least for the time being, there is a high degree of consensus around these goals, and agreement that there are no major impediments to their attainment. Consensus does not have to be built; a shared identity and a sense of unity are common property. While there are elements of discrimination and negative stereotyping (see Chapter 3), they have not been embodied in deeply irrational animosities or rigid institutional barriers. Cohesiveness—a key term in much of the theorizing about integration—does not, in the Israeli context, always have the American connotation of the necessity for *creating* bonds of relationship and commitment before new behavior can take place. Instead, for many tasks and settings, the unifying theme is present to begin with and allows for rapid agreement on working toward given goals. Much will depend, therefore, on how a particular setting will invoke and mobilize the underlying unity, as well as on providing the technical means for effective participation.

American theorists have stressed in their work the optimal, even ideal, conditions for the "successful" impact of integration, drawing on laboratory models and experimental settings (youth centers, summer camps) for their data and conclusions. It is quite possible, however, that the dynamics of group formation and interpersonal influence in such settings are not identical with those of the school classroom. Pupils do not generally choose of their own free will to be in school. They do not have the option of leaving the group whenever they want, or have much say in changing its leadership or power structure. The threat of dissolution—which makes the issue of cohesiveness so critical in voluntary groups—is not a major issue in classrooms. The central activity of the school, particularly in Israel, is the transmission of knowledge. Whether or not the classroom forms a "true" social unit is only a secondary consideration in evaluating the success or failure of teachers and pupils. The results of our study (i.e., improved academic achievement of disadvantaged children in integrated settings with special provision for the teaching and learning problems involved, and without major changes in personal attributions or classroom status) suggest a more modest and proximally oriented way of asking questions of how and why. Are there *minimal* organizational, social, and motivational conditions that can be met so that (a) the organizational integrity of the classroom is maintained; (b) there is no mutual rejection by the groups involved around central academic tasks; (c) a necessary level of motivation in the disadvantaged group is sustained; and (d) a context for learning defined by the behavioral and achievement norms of the majority is developed?

These questions do not touch on problems of equal status or major alterations of self-perception. The elementary school classroom is not seen as the arena for undoing historical discrimination or of totally modeling a remedy for social injustice. In keeping with the analysis of the meaning of the term *integration* in the Israeli context, the classroom issue is better defined in terms of assimilation. The aim is to induct a disadvantaged minority group into ways of thinking and behaving characteristic of Western culture and basic to the educational system. This is clearly an asymmetrical goal: One group emulates another. The majority group is not required to change much of its own behavior or norms, or become more like the minority. The problem is one of coordinating different processes taking place simultaneously in the total group. As in a theater, all the participants—teacher, minority group children, majority group children—must play out their required and different roles if there is to be a "successful" performance. The inability, reluctance, or refusal to play the assigned part by any of the participants will seriously affect the others and threaten the integrity of the whole. We will suggest in what follows some of the more prominent features of such performances characteristic of each of the major participants.

The Majority Group

Many researchers on integration hold that *classroom social atmosphere* is the most important element in the disadvantaged child's "success" (Gerard, Jackson, & Conolley, 1975). However, a classroom atmosphere that is accepting of disadvantaged children may not necessarily require the majority child's viewing his minority peer as equal to him either in ability or status. It may be enough for the majority group to provide what can be called "tolerant" behavior, and thus not put obstacles in the way of serving as a positive reference group of membership (Hyman, 1942).

In a number of conversations carried out by the authors with teachers participating in the research project, the topic of tolerance was usually spoken of in two ways. One was simply the readiness to behave politely with minority children, and to refrain from doing or saying things that could be intepreted as implying rejection or dislike. The socialization of the middle-class child usually includes an early introduction to the role of the sociable peer. He or she learns fairly early how not to respond impulsively and in open criticism of others, to minimize conflicts of all sorts, and to distinguish between public and private realms of action and discourse. Put another way, "successful" classrooms in the study may have been those where the majority of pupils had the social sophistication to enable them (under appropriate conditions of adult leadership and support) to play the pupil role in such a way as to allow smooth social functioning, despite significant intergroup differences. This does not mean that differences suddenly disappeared or that the middle-class child was not aware of them. Under certain conditions, however, he or she might be willing to ignore or at least not place much public emphasis on these differences in his or her daily contacts with the minority child.

Tolerance was also given another definition by the teachers: allowing the minority group the feeling that they can somehow cross the social barrier and join the majority. This feeling is probably connected to the behavioral models presented by the majority in learning activities and in classroom relationships, as well as the opportunities for adoption of these behaviors by the minority and their positive reinforcement and recognition.

The Minority Group

Teachers were often convinced that the primary motivation of the disadvantaged children as they began school was the simple wish to belong. The integration process for the minority group began with accepting majority group members as models for identification, and trying to imitate these models so as to be more like them, and be accepted by them. As the minority child adopted desirable behaviors, he became eligible for evaluative rewards and the consent of his middle-class peers to participate in their activities and games. Even where this agreement was mainly that of tolerance or the reserved expression of ordinary politeness, it was probably enough to give the disadvantaged child the impression that acceptance is not impossible (at least in some fields).

This, of course, is quite different from the classical social psychological position requiring the subgroups involved in the formation of a single cohesive group to share common goals, and to realize that these goals will not be achieved without the union of each subgroup's resources and energies with those of the other (Allport, 1954; Amir, 1969). It appears that a minimal condition for "successful" integration of two groups that differ significantly on social, cultural, and intellectual dimensions is the readiness of the minority to "assimilate" with the majority and to adopt its behavior, customs, and style of relating. Another way of putting this is to view "successful" integration as a situation where the majority maintains its status and most of its basic goals while "allowing" the minority members to forego something of their own style and, in its place, to adopt that of the majority. This is perhaps less a psychological principle than it is a way of restating major themes in Israeli social policy and ideology. Support in the wider society for such an approach, however, is probably critical for its effective implementation in the classroom.

Our analysis suggests that the middle-class group's perception of the difference between the groups is more critical than that of the lower-class children. A majority view of lower-class children as irremediably different (and acting on this perception) must be centrally involved in feelings of rejection and the denial of any hope of belonging on the part of the lower-class child. On the other hand, the lower-class children's awareness that there is a significant difference between them and their classmates does not necessarily have to lead to a sense of frustration and failure. What is important is whether or not minority children are consistently enabled and rewarded in their efforts to fulfill the pupil role as defined by the teacher and the majority group.

These rewards must afford the disadvantaged child a sense of competence and progress in those areas which are known to all to be the most relevant in the classroom. Looking at the situation this way only underlines the fact that there are several dimensions to the differences between the groups, and that the intellectual difference alone does not have to dictate whether or not integration is successful. The gap between the subgroups will be problematic when the disadvantaged children do not want, or are either incapable of or not encouraged, to respond in such a way as to earn positive reward from the majority. The gap will also be problematic when the majority is rewarded for rejecting behaviors by teachers, parents, and/or the organization of the school experience (i.e., when they do not successfully carry out the tolerance game).

The Teacher

One of the more widely circulated interpretations of Coleman's (1966) data holds that the teacher makes an insignificant contribution to the improved achievement of the disadvantaged (Grant,

1972). It is difficult to see how this conclusion can in any way be inferred from what actually takes place in the integrated classroom. Our experience in this study strongly suggests that the teacher plays a critical role in the creation and enhancement of an appropriate social framework that can productively contain two differing subgroups. Without the teacher's leadership and support, we doubt if pupils would be capable of overcoming the tensions and problems of integration and keep them from bursting into open conflict.

In the classroom comprised only of disadvantaged children, almost all the demand and reward for desired behavior must come from the teacher, without much support or assistance from the pupils. The integrated classroom, on the other hand, potentially contains a large number of socializing agents who can both serve as models and provide rewards that tie directly into the motives and needs of the minority children. Just quantitatively, the number of reinforcements that can be delivered by peers both during classroom hours (given an appropriate organization of setting) and during recesses is much greater than what the teacher can give any particular pupil under normal classroom procedure. The teacher can take advantage of this opportunity by providing many opportunities for appropriate behaviors and rewards, and by limiting the expression of intolerance and rejection. Conversely, if the teacher explicitly or implicitly sanctions discriminatory and rejecting behavior, there is little or no chance that the disadvantaged children will come to see themselves as part of the classroom group, or gain any meaningful benefit from the academic advantages potentially available in the integrated setting (Johnson, Gerard, & Miller, 1975).

The significance of the interaction found in our study between integrated setting and special educational intervention in affecting the lower-class children's academic achievement can now be reiterated. Along with providing specific academic input, the special program helped the teacher mobilize many opportunities for social interaction, the initiation and display of praiseworthy behaviors, and, not infrequently, cooperative dependence. Learning and social participation were brought together in at least an approximation of a complementary relationship—strikingly different from other "integrated" classrooms where the two remained separate, if not antagonistic. The combination of a high-status setting enhancing the normative features of the majority *and* the technical means of providing meaningful participation for the minority on school-relevant tasks was critical. It is in this sense, however, that it is also a fragile construction. Building and maintaining such a setting is highly dependent on teacher training, sophistication, and beliefs; on continued support and input from educational authorities; and on tacit, if not explicit, agreement in the community that such programs are possible. Serious deficiencies in any of these areas must lead to a deterioration of whatever effectiveness might be gained.

Internalization and Integration

Are the kinds of processes we have just sketched what is really meant by integration? Is imitation of others' behavior a rather superficial and perhaps undesirable change in the value system of the disadvantaged child? Does encouraging tolerance and "as-if" equitable behaviors on the part of the middle-class child fit with broader educational and social goals?

There is no easy way to answer these questions except to raise again the issue of proximal versus distal goals. In all that we have written there is an assumption that focusing on what is immediately and modestly attainable in the classroom may be a step in the direction of a more all-inclusive vision. The emphasis is on modeling and active role entry as important elements in the adoption of certain norms of work and behavior. These changes, in turn, may be critical for greater academic success, even in the absence of basic personality alteration. The classroom may bring to bear a variety of influences and experiences to encourage the adoption of new behaviors. These influences and experiences, however, are linked to what schools can do, rather than the attempt to create a miniature version of ultimate goals. Thus, "learning the rules of the game" may effectively contribute to improved academic outcome, even in the presence of large and continuing differences between the subgroups.

Perhaps this more developmental view can be taken only where there is agreement in the wider society that there are no major impediments to mobility, and where a basic unity of purpose and identity helps to downplay antagonisms born of differences. Under such conditions, there are few signs of that pressure to turn the school into an arena where majority and minority must "rethink their historical relationship to one another," or "feel more of a stake in each other's well-being than they have in the past [Jencks,

1972]." There is no guarantee that everyday classroom issues of tolerance, joint effort, and accrual of learning will lead to a more equitable future. However, it seems plausible and fits well with a general pattern of beliefs held by the wider society.

Our suggestion of a kind of "theater of equality," where children and teachers fill minimal role requirements in order to increase the assimilatory impact of the school, may begin to break down under at least two sets of conditions. One is a disturbance of national consensus, such that faith in achieving unity is questioned, symbols of shared national identity begin to lose their power, and serious concerns are raised about the psychological and social costs of forcing contact and change. A second possible condition is where the assimilatory focus turns distasteful, as when issues of minority group pride and identity become increasingly prominent. In both these circumstances, distal goals are likely to become everyday school issues. More attention will be paid to how well the school experience can approximate "ultimate" goals, and more stress will be placed on indicators—status differences, mutual dependence, attitudes, and personality change—thought to be directly related to such an approximation. The more proximal goals of the classroom may become secondary, and even irrelevant (Jencks, 1972). Developments such as these can contribute to a situation where issues, once otherwise taken for granted, are questioned, publicized, analyzed, and debated. Several different points of view about school integration in Israel are now battling for prominence. The approach highlighted in this book places a premium on the development of more effective teaching and learning methods in integrated classrooms, but it is by no means the most prevalent or popular. Another holds that school integration is an end in itself: Every disadvantaged child has the right to obtain all the benefits enjoyed by middle-class pupils, and these benefits are most readily available in integrated schools.

However, research findings suggesting that integration in itself does not contribute to positive outcomes, either academic or social, present a major dilemma. Curiously enough, one stance then taken is to reiterate even more loudly and emphatically the need to implement integration "at any price." But this position, with its suggestion of a possible loss of some participants, is difficult to defend publicly. It is therefore interesting to note a recent trend toward interpreting no negative effects of integration programs as a positive result. For example, the fact that no differences were found in the achievement of children of Asian–African origin in integrated junior high schools as compared to similar children in 8-year elementary schools (Chen *et al.,* 1978) is taken as a positive development. No decrement in performance after integration is regarded as an achievement in itself, even though this is an ex-post-facto argument not to be found in the original intent of the program. Changing the rules of the game in this fashion suggests that social, political, and ideological aspects of the school integration issue are becoming more salient and outspoken than ever before, with educational issues receding in importance.

It is this last possibility that presents a major problem for those who, like the authors, believe that integrated classrooms can be an effective setting for educational intervention.

Integration in Elementary and High Schools

A third set of conditions, relatively independent of major changes in social context and belief, can also be described. This turns on the little-discussed differences in implementation of school integration programs at the high school versus elementary school level. The impression in the literature on integration is that basically the same operations can be carried out at various age levels and in various settings. This fails to take into account developmental features which may require different models and different approaches.

Elementary school age children are limited in the number of categories and concepts they bring to social and authority relationships, and to problems of self and goal definition. They are usually remarkably pliable and open to situations of social influence, with the world of the school fairly representative of what they can grasp and categorize elsewhere. Their demands for personal and social reward tend also to be very present-oriented and not very sophisticated, a situation easily capitalized on by the kind of "tolerance" behavior we have already described. The school in a very real sense is their world, offering either confirmation of what they already know about themselves, or some new ideas and possibilities which, because of the powerful way they are presented, are alternatively acceptable. Furthermore, their perception of themselves as a social beings (rather than personal family members) is almost completely limited to those categories of feeling and relationships defined by teachers, school peers, and the behavioral universe they create. This social perception is still quite crude, however; it will not take much to make them feel similar and accepted, or, conversely, different and excluded. Nor does the personal pay-off have to be very great; they will be attuned to concrete examples of acceptance, and not very sophisticated about (or cognitively able to be sensitive to) "deep" and subtle meanings and attitudes.

Adolescents, however, are sensitive to a much wider range of intellectual, social, and moral differences. They can subject their experiences to increasingly more differentiated analyses and judgments. As a result, they are much more aware of duplicity, just as they are no longer willing to accept authority merely because someone fills a position. Their world often presents situations and personal feed-back in marked contrast to what is officially and academically announced to them. They may superficially accept a given situation because of a judgment of pay-off or superior power, but these perceptions no longer necessarily lead to acquiescence or identification. Moreover, both their fields of action and time perspectives have widened to include considerations of their own futures and the various activities and subroles that will bring them closer to what they will be as adults.

In other words, the "facts" of an integration program can be processed differently at different ages—the same operations may have quite different meanings and effects in elementary and high school settings. Young children may be relatively easily impressed with or accede to concrete, organizational signs of "acceptance" even if they are not completely meant. They are not necessarily uncomfortable with hidden meanings and discrepancies, nor are they heavily involved in making cross-comparisons with other aspects of their experiences or future prospects. Moreover, young disadvantaged children may not know, as we do from many conversations, that many of their teachers *in private* are not terribly hopeful about their prospects or talents. Nor are they aware that many of their peers go to their middle-class homes to talk with their parents about their schoolmates' clumsiness or ineptitude.

The increased cognitive sophistication and enlarged social world of the adolescent, however, mean that actions are not always taken at face value. The expanded world of the adolescent and the high school means that there will be many more opportunities for testing how seriously intentions are meant—and that many more chances for discrepancies will arise. In order for "tolerance" to have anything like the impact it can have on an elementary level, it must become *politically* real to the adolescent—and by *political* we mean the conscious and everyday dealing with moral issues that concern the relationships among people. Questions of social justice, responsibility, fairness, respect, cooperation, future role and status are all salient and important to the adolescent, who is much too sophisticated (no matter what his or her IQ) to simply accept being told "we are all equal here" while much of everyday experience, both in and out of school, proves otherwise (see Bidwell [1972] for an extended discussion of this point).

Clearly, at the high school level, this is no longer just a problem of the disadvantaged minority student. Consider, for example, the way a ninth-grade middle-class student in an integrated junior high school in Jerusalem sees it:

> Everybody knows that the ones chosen for vocational school are dummies, and almost all of them are *Frechim*[3].... There is a line between us and them, and no one crosses it ... we were supposed to be "united" in this school, but whoever thought that would happen is just stupid.... They [the girls] dress like prostitutes. We'd never be caught dressed like that.... One of "them" is in our group, but he's different. He's talented and smart and does not talk with an *Ayin* or a *Chet*[4] and he's not "dark".... You can't change the system—that's just the way life is ....

Attitudes, such as those quoted above, indicate that the problem is not just in getting one group to change, but, and particularly at the high school level, all the children. In adolescence, attitudes and behaviors jell into norms that intensify distinctions and distance, rationalizing likes and dislikes into complex patterns of what is socially approved or disapproved. For the majority to begin in any way to serve as a normative reference group, their own attitudes and behaviors need to be called into question, and not just in the direction of simple politeness.

By contrast, the elementary school setting in Israel is, in an important sense, removed from critical aspects of social reality. Issues of success and failure are not sharply defined and, for the most

[3]A derogatory slang term often applied to children of Asian–African origin.
[4]This refers to a distinctive way of pronouncing Hebrew letters characteristic of the speech of children of Asian–African origin.

part, all children will "make it" through the system. The Israeli high school, on the other hand, with its high standards of academic success clearly linked to social and institutional referents like university admissions, army placement, occupation, and so on, offers little relief or escape. Distal goals and concerns become prominent, everyday issues. The very organization of the school emphasizes group differences while providing very few opportunities for improvement and advancement. The School Reform Program in Israel was an attempt to recognize the link between the organizational structure of the schools and its effects on different groups of pupils, as well as to try and do something about it. Israeli researchers (Chen *et al.*, 1975) have shown how many of the comprehensive schools brought into being by the School Reform Program have managed to reinstate elements of separation and differentiation—elements they were supposedly created to do away with (see Rosenbaum & Presser [1978] for an interesting American example of a similar process).

Integration at the high school level may, therefore, have to be much more radical, educationally and organizationally, than has been considered or implemented up until now. The option we described for the elementary school—focusing on proximal matters in the classroom along with mobilizing the appearances of solidarity and collective action—may not be as applicable at older ages. To even begin to create the special group atmosphere held necessary for reinforcing change, important alterations in self-perception and interpersonal relationships must be made. Here the models stressing such changes become more salient. Still, we have pointed out how transferring such models from the laboratory to actual schools probably involves a degree of institutional, as well as political restructuring whose actual dimensions have yet to be explored.[5]

A Final Word

In school, as in church, we deal with the world that we wish existed, trying to inspire our descendents with ideals we ourselves have failed to live up to. We assume, for example, that there is no chance of making adults live together in desegregated neighborhoods, so we try to impose this ideal on

[5]All of this holds true as far as the Jewish population of Israel is concerned. Still to be confronted is the much more complex issue of integration with the Arab population.

children by inventing elaborate school busing plans. If as we argue ... intellectual and moral experiments on children have little effect on adult life, many people are likely to lose interest in schools. Children per se do not interest them very much [Jencks *et al.*, 1972, p. 260].

Jencks boldly asserted this in the process of questioning whether schools have anything to contribute to social change—particularly, to making adults more equal. The quotation is a useful illustration of the point we have been trying to make in these final pages: Any particular instance of school integration is a dynamic, shifting configuration of forces, meanings, and actual practices, with universal laws and operations probably few and far between.

Jencks's own words, for example, need to be seen against a background of a steady escalation in the debate around integration in the United States. This debate has followed a trajectory from rather simple beliefs in the efficacy of educational intervention through a growing distrust and questioning of the whole enterprise. The most prominent feeling in the Jencks quotation is one of qualified despair—over the discrepancy between real and ideal worlds, and particularly over the ability of schools to play anything like a significant role in reducing such discrepancies. The perceived failure of the schools to make a noticeable difference in the lives of children is measured against wide-ranging failures in adult society, and thus found extremely wanting. The implication is that the educational process itself and all its various spin-offs—knowledge, acculturation, achievement, certification, and so on—can hardly bring about a better world. There is the suggestion that faith in schools and children as agents of social change is only a transitory phenomenon. The last is particularly surprising in a country that fostered the growth of the most pervasive of modern pedagogical theories, one that precisely centered on the revolutionary potential of children and their education.

Many have argued with the substance of Jencks's point of view (Levine & Bane, 1975), but the feelings of disappointment, of complexity, and of questioning the basic correctness of the idea are widespread. Meanings have changed:

As a result of the school desegregation process following *Brown,* blacks developed a more refined sense of radical injustice in the schools, a much decreased willingness to stand the pain, and a sharply reduced appetite for white people's solutions. All of this worked a change in social reality; what

would have been an entirely acceptable integrated high school in 1954
would have seemed an outrageous insult in 1974 [Cohen & Weiss, 1977, p.
398].

As definitions shift, the lists of "things to do" in order to implement
integration programs become longer and often contradictory (St.
John, 1975, Chapter 6). Despite continued calls for detailed examination of actual school experience, and for altering the educational
process itself, very little is done. Survey studies and regression
analyses repeatedly highlight how the major share of the variance
in academic achievement is limited to home background. Few experimental studies, however—such as reported in our work—are
carried out to probe what schools could accomplish within the limits
of their possible impact. More skepticism is raised about current
theories of change (Gerard & Miller, 1975), but little is offered to
replace them.

The situation in Israel, as we have tried to point out, offers an
interesting contrast. Ethnic and class differences are muted, and the
need for total mobilization and unity is still prominent. While there
is a nagging sense of incompleteness in the attainment of national
goals, there are no deeply irrational forces and antagonisms to overcome. Faith in education—both as an end in itself (a traditional
Jewish value) and as a means for social mobility and change—
remains central. Achievement and certification do make a difference in a country still struggling for a competitive position na-
tionally, economically, and technologically. The readiness to carry
out "intellectual and moral experiments" with children, while
somewhat tempered by research results, has not appreciably abated.
The kind of model for school integration we have suggested, and the
results obtained in our study, derive their significance from the
supports and consensus available in the wider society—and probably cannot be understood apart from them.

But we have also said that any given instance or model of school
integration is a fragile construction. The experimental schools in
our study, for example, are fighting to maintain their effectiveness.
Population shifts, budget cuts, inadequate teacher preparation—all
have had their effects. Special classes and "groupings" have begun
to appear where once they would have been dismissed as inappropriate. Education authorities have not invested in preparing materials and techniques for integrated classrooms, and many of the

intuitively gained approaches learned from the project schools have all but disappeared from practice.

Moreover, the debate on integration in Israel has begun to take a qualitative turn. This can be seen as part of a general trend in contemporary Israeli society where there are signs of breakdown in older styles of consensus. A plurality of interests that rapidly emerged following the October War of 1973 are no longer easily contained by traditional symbols and slogans. In the case of school integration, there is no retreat from belief in the value and efficacy of education. However, occasional parent strikes, disappointing results of research studies, wide press and TV coverage, and government investigatory commissions have all contributed to changing the terms of the argument, complicating and raising doubts about what was once a relative uniformity of opinion. Demands for recognition of ethnic identity and pride are beginning to be heard. Where once issues of personality and group change were of secondary concern, they are increasingly thrust into prominence as different, sometimes antagonistic, community interests battle for legitimacy. The experimental project we have described already appears to many educators as a rather simple way of doing things when compared to the current situation.

The shifts and alterations in what school integration is all about underline the inadequacy of searching for a single set of explanatory principles or techniques. Schools can make a difference, but only when attention is paid to the everyday life of classrooms, and all those in them and around them who must daily recreate the conditions for learning. It is these continuous acts of making, building, and even occasionally destroying, that need to be understood, and certainly not alone by the psychological perspective to which we have mostly limited ourselves. We have not—indeed, cannot—come up with an answer; we hope we have indicated some useful directions.

References

Adar, Z. Critique of the national educational curriculum. *Megamot,* 1956, *7,* 41–49 (Hebrew).

Allport, G. W. *The nature of prejudice.* Cambridge, Mass.: Addison Wesley, 1954.

Amir, Y. Contact hypothesis in ethnic relations. *Psychological Bulletin,* 1969, *71,* 319–342.

Amir, Y. The role of inter-group contact in change of prejudice and ethnic relations. In P. A. Katz (Ed.), *Towards the elimination of racism.* New York: Pergamon Press, 1976. Pp. 245–308.

Amir, Y., Rich, Y., & Ben Ari, R. Problems of social integration in junior high school, gain and loss to pupils, and proposed solutions. *Studies in Education,* 1978, *18,* 15–36 (Hebrew).

Amir, Y., Sharan, S., Bizman, A., Rivner, M., & Ben-Ari, R. Personal and group factors in change of ethnic attitudes of students in Israeli high schools. *Megamot,* 1977, *23,* 174–188 (Hebrew).

Andrea, J. The three stages of opening a classroom. In C. E. Silberman (Ed.), *The open classroom reader.* New York: Random House, 1973. Pp. 462–467.

Aronson, E., Blaney, N., Sikes, J., Stephan, C., & Snapp, M. Busing and racial tension, the jigsaw route to learning and liking. *Psychology Today,* 1975, *8,* 43–50.

Aronson, E., Stephan, C., Sikes, J., Blaney, N., & Snapp, M. *The jigsaw classroom.* Beverly Hills, Calif.: Sage Publications, 1978.

Ausubel, D. P., & Ausubel, P. Ego development among segregated Negro children. In H. A. Passow (Ed.), *Education in depressed areas.* New York: Bureau of Publications, Teacher's College, Columbia University, 1963. Pp. 109–141.

Averch, H. A., Carroll, S. J., Donaldson, T. S., Kiesling, H. J., & Pricus, J. How effective is schooling? A critical synthesis and review of research findings. In D. M. Levine & M. J. Bane (Eds.), *The "inequality" controversy: Schooling and distributive justice.* New York: Basic Books, 1975. Pp. 63–97.

Bachman, J. G., & O'Mally, P. M. Self-esteem in young men: A longitudinal analysis of the impact of education and occupational attainment. *Journal of Personality and Social Psychology,* 1977, *35,* 365–380.

Bartel, H. W., Bartel, N. R., & Grill, J. J. A sociometric view of some integrated open classrooms. *Journal of Social Issues,* 1973, *29,* 159–173.

Bereiter, C., & Englemann, S. *Teaching disadvantaged children in the preschool.* Englewood Cliffs, N.J.: Prentice Hall, 1966.

Berger, P. L., Berger, B., & Kellner, H. *The homeless mind.* New York: Random House, 1973.

Bidwell, C. E. Schooling and socialization for moral commitment. *Interchange,* 1972, *3–4,* 1–27.

Binyamini, K., & Sherf, T. Educational expectations and teacher's experience: A case study of psychological change processes in the school. *Megamot,* 1977, *23,* 209–220 (Hebrew).

Blaney, N. T., Stephan, C., Rosenfield, D., Aronson, E., & Sikes, J. Interdependence in the classroom: A field study. *Journal of Educational Psychology,* 1977, *69,* 121–128.

Bradley, L. A., & Bradley, G. W. The academic achievement of black students in desegregated schools: A critical review. *Review of Educational Research,* 1977, *47,* 399–449.

Bridgeman, B., & Shipman, V. C. *Predictive value of measures of self-esteem and achievement motivation in four-to-nine year old low-income children.* Princeton, N.J.: Educational Testing Service, 1975.

Bridgeman, B., & Shipman, V. C. Preschool measure of self-esteem and achievement motivation as predictors of third grade achievement. *Journal of Educational Psychology,* 1978, *70,* 17–28.

Bronfenbrenner, U. Toward an experimental ecology of human development. *American Psychologist,* 1977, *32,* 513–531.

Brookover, W. B., & Thomas, S. Self-concept of ability and school achievement. *Sociology of Education,* 1964, *37,* 271–278.

Calsyn, R. J., & Kenny, D. A. Self-concept of ability and perceived evaluation of others: Cause or effect of academic achievement? *Journal of Educational Psychology,* 1977, *69,* 136–145.

Campbell, D. T., & Boruch, R. F. Making the case for randomized assignment to treatments by considering the alternatives: Six ways in which quasi-experimental evaluations in compensatory education tend to underestimate effects. In C. A. Bennett & A. A. Lumsdaine (Eds.), *Evaluation and experiment: Some critical issues in assessing social programs.* New York: Academic Press, 1975. Pp. 195–284.

Chen, M., Kfir, D., & Fresco, B., *Coping with a heterogeneous student body in integrated schools.* Tel Aviv: Tel Aviv University, 1975.

Chen, M., Lewy, A., & Adler, C. *Educational process and outcome: Evaluation of the junior-high school reform.* Jerusalem: Ministry of Education, 1978 (Hebrew).

Chen, M., Lewy, A., & Kfir, D. The possibilities of interethnic group contact in the junior high schools: Implementation and results. *Megamot*, 1977, *23*, 101–123 (Hebrew).

Cicirelli, V. G. Relationship of socioeconomic status and ethnicity to primary grade children's self-concept. *Psychology in the Schools*, 1977, *14*, 213–215.

Clark, K. B. Educational stimulation of racially disadvantaged children In A. H. Passow (Ed.), *Education in depressed areas*. New York: Teachers College Press, Columbia University, 1963. Pp. 142–162.

Cohen, D. K. & Garet, M. Reforming educational policy with applied research. *Harvard Educational Review*, 1975, *45*, 17–43.

Cohen, D. K., & Weiss, J. A. Social science and social policy: Schools and race. *The Educational Forum*, 1977 (May), 394–413.

Cohen, E. G. The effects of desegregation on race relations. *Law and Contemporary Problems*, 1975, *33*, 271–299.

Cohen, E. G., Lockheed, M. E., & Lohman, M. R. The center for interracial cooperation: A field experiment. *Sociology of Education*, 1976, *49*, 47–58.

Coleman, J. S., Campbell, E. R., Hobson, C. J., McPartland, J., Mood, A. M., Wernfield, F. D., & York, R. L. *Equality of educational opportunities*. Washington, D.C.: U.S. Government Printing Office, 1966.

Coleman, J. S. Methods and results in the IEA studies of effects of school on learning. *Review of Educational Research*, 1975, *75*, 355–386.

Cook, S. W. Desegregation: A psychological analysis. In W. W. Charters, Jr. & N. L. Gage (Eds.), *Reading in the social psychology of education*. Boston: Allyn and Bacon, 1963. Pp. 40–50.

Cook, S. W. Social science and school desegregation: Did we mislead the Supreme Court? *Personality and Social Psychology Bulletin*, 1979, *5*, 420–437.

Cook, T. D., & Campbell, D. T. The design and conduct of quasi-experimental and true experiments in field settings. In M. D. Dunnette (Ed.), *Handbook of industrial and organizational research*. New York: Rand McNally, 1976. Pp. 223–326.

Crain, R. L., & Mahard, R. E. Desegregation and black achievement: A review of the research. *Law and Contemporary Problems*, 1978, *42*, 17–56.

Cronbach, L. J. Beyond the two disciplines of scientific psychology. *American Psychologist*, 1975, *30*, 1–14.

Deutsch, M. *Minority group and class status as related to social and personality factors in scholastic achievement*. Ithaca, N.Y.: Cornell University Press, 1960.

DeVries, D. L., Edwards, K. J., & Slavin, R. E. Biracial teams and race relations in the classroom: Four field experiments using teams–games–tournament. *Journal of Educational Psychology*, 1978, *70*, 356–362.

Dunn, C., & Payne, B. *The effects of group guidance upon the self esteem, interpersonal relationships and educational achevement of the culturally different child*. Houston, Texas: University of Houston, 1969.

Eisenstadt, S. N. *Israeli society*. London: Weidenfeld and Nicholson, 1967.

Eisenstadt, S. N. Change and continuity in Israeli society. *The Jerusalem Quarterly*, 1977, *2* (Winter), 3–11.

Epps, E. G. Impact of school desegregation on aspirations, self-concepts and other aspects of personality. *Law and Contemporary Problems*, 1975, *39*, 300–313.

Eshel, Y. Antecedents of academic success and failure: Re-examination of current criteria of disadvantage. *Studies in Education,* in press. (Hebrew.)

Epps, E. G. The impact of school segregation on the self-evaluation and achievement orientation of minority children. *Law and Contemporary Problems,* 1978, *42* (3), 57–76.

Eshel, Y., & Klein, Z. School integration, academic self-image, and achievement of lower-class elementary school pupils. *Megamot,* 1977, *23,* 134–145 (Hebrew).

Eshel, Y., & Klein, Z. The effects of integration and open education on mathematics achievement in the early primary grades in Israel. *American Educational Research Journal,* 1978, *15,* 319–323.

Evans, M. A. A comparative study of young children's classroom activities and learning outcomes. *British Journal of Educational Psychology,* 1979, *49,* 15–26.

Forehand, J. A., & Ragosta, M. *A handbook for integrated schooling.* Princeton, N.J.: Educational Testing Service, 1976.

Foreman, S. G., & McKinney, J. D. Creativity and achievement of second graders in open and traditional classrooms. *Journal of Educational Psychology,* 1978, *70,* 101–107.

Frankenstein, C. The complexity of the concept of integration. In C. Frankenstein (Ed.), *Teaching as a social challenge.* Jerusalem: Sivan Press, 1976. Pp. 137–159.

Frey, W. H. Central city white flight: Racial and non-racial causes. *American Sociological Review,* 1979, *44,* 425–448.

Gerard, H. B., Jackson, T. D., & Conolley, E. S. Social contact in the desegregated classroom. In H. B. Gerard & N. Miller, *School desegregation.* New York: Plenum, 1975. Pp. 211–241.

Gerard, H. B., & Miller, N. *School desegregation.* New York: Plenum, 1975.

Gergen, K. J., & Marececk, J. *Psychology of self-esteem.* Morristown, N.J.: General Learning Press, 1976.

Gibbey, R. J., & Gabler, R. The self-concept of Negro and white children. *Journal of Clinical Psychology,* 1967, *23,* 144–150.

Goldstein, S. Judicial intervention in educational decision making: An Israeli-American comparison. In S. Goldstein (Ed.), *Education, law and equality.* Jerusalem: Van Leer Jerusalem Foundation, in press.

Grant, G. On equality of educational opportunities. *Harvard Educational Review,* 1972, *42,* 109–125.

Hallinan, T. M. Friendship patterns in open and traditional classrooms. *Sociology of Education,* 1976, *49,* 254–265.

Hill, B. V. What's "open" about open education? In D. Nyberg (Ed.), *The philosophy of open education.* London: Routledge and Kegan Paul, 1975. Pp. 3–13.

Horowitz, R. A. Psychological effects of the 'open classroom.' *Review of Educational Research,* 1979, *49,* 71–86.

Hyman, H. H. The psychology of status. *Archives of Psychology,* 1942, *269,* 269–284.

Inbar, M., & Adler, C. *Ethnic integration in Israel: A case study of Moroccan brothers who settled in France and Israel.* New Brunswick, N.J.: Transaction Books, 1977.

Irwin, F. S. Sentence completion responses and scholastic success or failure. *Journal of Consulting Psychology,* 1967, *14,* 269–271.

Israel Ministry of Education and Culture. Trends in activity based education. *Bachinuch Hayesodi,* Publication No. 12, Jerusalem, 1973 (Hebrew).

Israel Ministry of Education and Culture.: The "activity" oriented classroom. *Bachinuch Hayesodi,* Jerusalem, 1978 (Hebrew).

Jencks, C., Smith M., Acland, H., Bane, M. G., Lohen, D., Gintis, H., Hyens, B., & Michelson, S. *Inequality: A reassessment of the effect of family and schooling in America.* New York: Harper and Row, 1972.

Johnson, E. B., Gerard, H. B., & Miller, N. Teacher influence in the desegregated classroom. In H. B. Gerard & N. Miller, *School integration.* New York: Plenum Press, 1975, Pp. 243–260.

Katz, I. Socialization of academic motivation. In D. Levine (Ed.), *Nebraska Symposium on motivation.* Lincoln, Neb.: University of Nebraska Press, 1967. Pp. 133–191.

Katz, I. Factors influencing performance in the desegregated school. In M. Deutsch, I. Katz & A. Jensen (Eds.), *Social class, race and psychological development.* New York: Holt, Rinehart, and Winston, 1968. Pp. 254–290.

Kifer, E. Relationships between academic achievement and personality characteristics: A quasi-longitudinal study. *American Educational Research Journal,* 1975, *12,* 191–210.

Klein, Z., & Eshel, Y. Towards a psycho-social definition of school integration. *Megamot,* 1977, *23,* 17–40 (Hebrew).

Klein, Z., & Eshel, Y. The open classroom in a cross-cultural perspective: A research note. *Sociology of Education,* in press.

Kleinberger, A. Reflections on equality in education. *Megamot* 1964, *13,* 257–288 (Hebrew).

Kleinberger, A. F. *Society, schools, and progress in Israel.* Oxford: Pergamon, 1969.

Kleinberger, A. Social integration as a main purpose and justification of the educational policy in Israel. *Beminhal Hachinuch* 1973, *3,* 11–24 (Hebrew).

Kozol, J. Free schools fail because they don't teach. *Psychology Today,* 1972, *5,* 30–36.

Lamm, Z. Social integration and educational policy. *Molad,* 1974, *25,* 589–596 (Hebrew).

Levin, J., & Chen, M. Sociometric choices in ethnically heterogeneous classes. *Megamot,* 1977, *23,* 189–208 (Hebrew).

Levine, D. M., & Bane, M. J. (Eds.). *The inequality controversy: Schooling and distributive justice.* New York: Harper and Row, 1975.

Lewin, K. *Dynamic theory of personality.* New York: McGraw-Hill, 1935.

McPartland, J. The relative influence of school and of classroom desegregation on the academic achievement of ninth grade Negro students. *Journal of Social Issues,* 1969, *25,* 93–102.

McPartland, J. M., & Epstein, J. L. Open schools and achievement: Extended tests of a finding of no relationship. *Sociology of Education,* 1977, *42,* 133–144.

Mead, G. H. *Mind, self and society.* Chicago: University of Chicago Press, 1934.

Miller, N. *Principles relevant to successful school desegregation.* Los Angeles: University of Southern California Press, 1977.

Miller, N., & Gerard, H. B. How busing failed in Riverside. *Psychology Today,* 1976, June, 66–100.

Minkovich, A. *Arithmetic achievement test for the first grade.* Jerusalem: Ministry of Education and Culture, 1968 (Hebrew).

Minkovich, A., Davis, D., & Bashi, J. *An evaluation study of Israeli elementary schools.* Jerusalem: Hebrew University, 1977.

Minuchin, P., Biber, B., Shapiro, E., & Zimiles, H. *The psychological impact of school.* New York: Basic Books, 1969.

Morse, W. C. Self-concept in the school setting. *Childhood Education.* 1964, *41,* 195–198.

Naftali, N. The activity oriented first grade. In: Israeli Ministry of Education and Culture, Trends in activity based education. *Bachinuch Hayesodi,* Publication No. 12, Jerusalem, 1973, 38–47 (Hebrew).

Orfield, G. How to make desegregation work: The adaptation of schools to their newly integrated student bodies. *Law and Contemporary Problems,* 1975, *39,* 314–340.

Ortar, G., & Ben-Shachar, N. *Reading comprehension test.* Jerusalem: Ministry of Education and Culture, 1972 (Hebrew).

Patchen, M., Hofmann, G., & Brown, W. R. Academic performance of black high school students under different conditions of contact with white peers. *Sociology of Education,* 1980, *53,* 33–51.

Peres, Y. Ethnic relations in Israel. *American Journal of Sociology,* 1971, *76,* 1021–1047.

Persitz, R. *Development of self-image among middle class and lower class elementary school pupils.* Unpublished M.A. dissertation, Hebrew University, Jerusalem, 1977.

Pettigrew, T. F., & Green, R. L. School desegregation in large cities: A critique of the Coleman "white flight" thesis. *Harvard Educational Review* 1976, *46,* 1–53.

Pettigrew, T. F., Useem, E., Norman, C., & Smith, M. Busing: A review of the evidence. *Public Interest,* 1973, *30,* 88–118.

Plowden Report. *Children and their primary schools.* London: Central Advisory Council for Education, H.M.S.O., 1967.

Porter, R. J. School desegregation: Outcomes for children by Nancy St. John (book review). *Harvard Educational Review,* 1976, *46,* 127–131.

Richer, S. Reference group theory and ability grouping: A convergence of sociological theory and educational research. *Sociology of Education,* 1976, *49,* 65–71.

Rist, R. C. Student social class and teacher expectations: The self-fulfilling prophecy in ghetto education. *Harvard Educational Review,* 1970, *40,* 411–451.

Rist, R. C. *The invisible children: School integration in American society.* Cambridge, Mass.: Harvard University Press, 1978.

Rogers, C., & Dymond, R. (Eds.) *Psychotherapy and personality change.* Chicago: University of Chicago Press, 1954.

Rosenbaum, J. E., & Presser, S. Voluntary racial integration in a magnet school. *School Review* (Feb.), 1978, *86,* 156–186.

Rosenberg, M., & Simmon, R. G. *Black and white self-esteem: The urban school child.* ASA Rose Monograph Series Publication. Washington, D. C.: American Sociological Association, 1972.

Rosenshine, B., & Furst, N. F. Performance criteria in teacher education. In B. O. Smith (Ed.), *Research on teacher education.* 1971. Pp. 38–72.

Rosenwald, G. C. Small group and the family. *Social Research* 1975, *42,* 247–283.

Rossell, C. R. School desegregation and community social change. *Law and Contemporary Problems,* 1978, *42* (3), 133–183.

Rubin, R. A., Dorle, J., & Sandidge, S. Self-esteem and school performance. *Psychology in the Schools,* 1977, *14,* 503–507.

Sarason, S. B. *The culture of the school and the problem of change.* Boston: Allyn and Bacon, 1971.

Scheirer, M. A., & Krant, R. E. Increasing educational achievement via self-concept change. *Review of Educational Research,* 1979, *49,* 131–150.

Schofield, J. School desegregation and intergroup relations. In D. Bar Tal & L. Saxe (Eds.), *Social psychology of education: Theory and research.* Washington, D.C.: Hemisphere Publishing Company, 1978. Pp. 329–363.

Schofield, J. W., & Sagar, H. A. Peer interaction in an integrated middle school. *Sociometry,* 1977, *40,* 130–138.

Sharan, S. Cooperative learning in small groups: Recent methods and effects on achievement, attitudes and ethnic relations, *Review of Educational Research,* 1980, *50,* 2, 241–271.

Sharan, S., Cohen, E., & Elchanani, D. Modifying status relations in Israel youth through expectation training. *Megamot,* 1977, *23,* 146–160 (Hebrew).

Sherf, T. *Stabilization and change of teacher expectations from first grade pupils, in the process of planned change in the school system.* Unpublished M.A. dissertation, Hebrew University, Jerusalem, 1973 (Hebrew).

Shuval, J. *Immigrants on the threshold.* New York: Atherton, 1963.

Silberman, C. E. (Ed.) *The open classroom reader.* New York: Vintage Books, 1973.

Singleton, L. C., & Asher, S. R. A developmental study of sociometric choices in integrated classroom. Paper presented at the annual meeting of the APA, San Francisco, August, 1977.

Slavin, R. E. Effects of bi-racial learning teams on cross-racial friendships. *Journal of Educational Psychology,* 1979, *71,* 381–387.

Stallings, J. Implementation and child effects of teaching practices in follow through classrooms. *Society for Research in Child Development Monographs.* 1975 (No. 163), Vol. 40.

Stenner, A. J. Self-concept development in young children. *Phi Delta Kappan,* 1976, *58,* 356–357.

Stephan, W. G. School desegregation: An evaluation of predictions made in Brown v. Board of Education. *Psychological Bulletin,* 1978, *85,* 217–238.

St. John, N. H. The elementary classroom as a frog-pond: Self-concept, sense of control and social context. *Social Forces,* 1971, *49,* 581–595.

St. John, N. H. *School desegregation outcomes for children.* New York: Wiley, 1975.

Stodolsky, S. S. Identifying and evaluating open education. *Phi Delta Kappan,* 1975, *57,* 113–117.

Tagiuri, P., Brunner, G. S., & Blake, R. R. On the relation between feelings and perception of feelings among members of small groups. In E. E. Maccoby, T. M. Newcomb, & E. L. Hartley (Eds.), *Readings in social psychology.* New York: Holt, Reinehart and Winston, 1958. Pp. 110–116.

Traub, R. E., Weiss, J., & Fisher, C. W. Studying openness in education: An Ontario example. *Journal of Research and Development in Education,* 1974, *8,* 47–59.

Traub, R. E., Weiss, J., Fisher, C. W., & Musella, D. Closure on openness: Describing and quantifying open education. *Interchange,* 1972, *3,* 69–83.

Walberg, H. J., & Thomas, S. C. Open education, an operational definition and validation in Great Britain and United States. *American Educational Research Journal,* 1972, *9,* 197–208.

Walberg, H. J., & Thomas, S. C. An analysis of American and British open education.

In B. Spodek & H. G. Walberg, (Eds.), *Studies in open education*. New York: Agathon Press, 1975. Pp. 143–154.

Ward, W. D., & Barcher, P. R. Reading achievement and creativity as related to open classroom experience. *Journal of Educational Psychology, 1975, 67,* 683–691.

Weber, L. *The English infant school and informal education.* Englewood Cliffs, N.J.: Prentice Hall, 1971.

Weinberg, M. The relationship between school desegregation and academic achievement: A review of the research. *Law and Contemporary Problems, 1975, 39,* 241–270.

Woock, R. R. Social perspective on desegregation policy and research. *Education and Urban Society, 1977, 9,* 385–394.

Wright, R. J. The affective and cognitive consequences of an open education elementary school. *American Educational Research Journal, 1975, 12,* 449–468.

Wylie, R. C. The present status of self theory. In E. F. Borgatta & W. W. Lambert (eds.), *Handbook of personality theory and research.* Chicago: Rand McNally & Co., 1968. Pp. 728–787.

Wylie, R. C. *The self-concept.* Lincoln, Neb.: University of Nebraska Press, 1974.

Wylie, R. C. *The self concept: A critical survey of pertinent research literature.* Lincoln, Neb.: University of Nebraska Press, 1961.

Yamamoto, K., Thomas, E., & Karnes, E. School related attitudes in middle-class school age students. *American Educational Research Journal, 1969, 6,* 191–206.

Subject Index

QUANTITATIVE STUDIES IN SOCIAL RELATIONS

Consulting Editor: Peter H. Rossi

UNIVERSITY OF MASSACHUSETTS
AMHERST, MASSACHUSETTS